"Like Whitman before him, Timothy Tarkelly takes anything and everything as his subject, and of particular interest to both poets is the human condition. The deep empathy Tarkelly shows the characters who populate his work anchors this collection, particularly in those poems he uses to examine his own past. But he's no narcissist, reserving the bulk of his attention for the world around him, even when he is present in a given poem, and that is one of his greatest strengths.

Another asset is the pure relatability of these pieces. Tarkelly's chosen topics range from history to religion, emotional health to love and longing, workaday life to consumerism—in other words, issues most of us grapple with every day. And he addresses them in language that is accessible to all: those who are new to poetry, those who have been reading verse for years, and even those who think they have no interest in the enterprise. Such a writer is a rare gem, and I propose that we keep this one in our collection."

-Caitlin Johnson, Author of *"Gods in the Wilderness"* and *"WAR/La Guerre"*

"There is an emotional breadth and depth to Tim's work that is palpable. A deep sense of abiding presence and immediacy felt in each poem; as if he's sitting there with you, across some table in a comfortable, darkened café. Two friends, swapping stories. Time well spent. And his words: the kind of intimate and profound vignettes about what colors our thoughts, holds our spirits captive, ruminates in the deepest parts of our mind."

-Vincent Larson, author of *"Ashtapadi: Webs of Light."*

"Tim Tarkelly's poetry is another example that the best poetry right now is coming out of the midwest. 21st-century modernist truths for a second lost generation who long for the little moments of life so they can yearn for more."

-Daniel W. Wright, Author of *"Brian Epstein Died for You"*

The You We Know and Love

New and Selected Poems
By Timothy Tarkelly

Spartan
Press

Spartan Press

Kansas City, Missouri

spartanpress.com

Spartan
Press

Copyright © Timothy Tarkelly, 2024

First Edition: 1 3 5 7 9 10 8 6 4 2

ISBN: 978-1-958182-60-4

LCCN: 2023952322

Cover photo: Bobby Clarkson

Title page image: Fatmah Al-Qadfan

Author photo: Caleb Wood

Acknowledgments:

Special thanks to the editor of the following publications where some of these poems first appeared (in some form or other):

"Somewhere Around Alva" - *Basset Hound Press*, "Collector's Edition" - *Unstamatic*, "Truly, I'd Punch Nineteen-Year-Old Me in the Face," "The Week Before I Got Sober... The First Time" - *Rusty Truck*, "How Did It Feel When You Deleted Our Photo Off of Your Instagram?" - *Back Patio Press*, "Hastings: A Remembrance," "The Baffled King" - *As It Ought To Be Magazine*, "Litany from a Facebook Post" - *Don't Submit!*, "Baptism" - *Work to a Calm*, "Georgia" - *Ablucionistas*, "I Regret Everything," "Soundless Tidings" - *Hamburger Channel*, "On Judging Found Notebooks by Their Covers," "Gospel Songs," "The Community" - *Floodlight Poetry*, "The Belle Fair" - *Flyover Country*, "Ten Chairs" - *The Red Lemon Review*, "Columbus," "Texas Martini," "Sunrise," "Jackie's Type," "Porching It Up," "Olathe," "Will You Sign My Yearbook," "Concerning Apocalypse," "OETR," "Rivertowne" - *The Great American Pyramid Scheme* (OAC Books), "Bargaining with Bad Luck" - *Words and Whispers*, "Swimming Hole" - *Plant People, an Anthology of Environmental Artists*, "Lighthouse" - *Jera Poems* (Roaring Junior Press), "Listening to Skip James" - *Detritus Online*, "My Zafu Is Collecting Dust" - *Amethyst Magazine*, "Codependence" - *Vocivia Magazine*, "Leaving Westford" - *Sledgehammer Lit*, "Iowa Workshop Model" - *Pulp Modern*, "Thirties" - *Philosophical Idiot*, "Lurasidone HCL," "Luckhound" - *Peculiars Magazine*, "Fingers" - *Vampcat Magazine*, "Writers Are Gods Here" - *Haunted Waters Press*, "Drinks with Old Friends" - *Ariel Chart*, "Maybe We Should Talk about the Bacchantes Always Being the Butt of a Joke When Really They Were Just Living Their Best Lives" - *Riggwelter*, "An Angel" - *Work to a Calm*, "Smarter After Midnight" "Have You Ever Seen a

Sunset?" - *Philosophical Idiot*, "Carnival of Souls" - *Vampcat Magazine*, "In My Memory, Things Always Happen in Winter," "Why Do You Act Like That?," "Apologies" - *Ariel Chart*, "Vermeer Watches Me Sleep," "Portrait of a Girl Dressed in Blue by Johannes Cornelisz Verspronk," "Open Letter to Winy Maas and the Residents of the Double House," "Girl with a Pearl Earring by Johannes Vermeer," "Scenes of Everyday Life," "Untitled" - *Objects We Know We Don't Deserve* (Alien Buddha Press), "Three Figures Near a Canal with Windmill by H.P. Bremmer" - *Wild Roof Journal*, "The Mondrian Collection By Yves Saint Lauren" - *Harpy Hybrid Review*, "AIT Thoughts" - *We Are Not Your Soldiers*, "First Steady Paycheck and He's Trolling" - *Rise Up Review*, "An Elegy for Industry," "A Statistic" - *Whisper and the Roar*, "Green" - *GNU*, "Maybe We Should Start a Poet's Bowling League" - *The Daily Drunk*, "Sea Legs" - *Gone Out Fishing* (Poet's Choice), "Dirt Dog" - *Lots of Light*, "Legal Sunrise" - *Agape Review*, "Live Up" - *Full House Literary Magazine*, "To Carlo and the Pope" - *Hollow Publishing*, "Six Shooter Blues" - *Typishly*

Table of Contents

"I had no interest in the revenge of living, only in being missed enough to be considered lost."

-Kat Giordano

For Erika Kim

I'M STILL SOBER, I PROMISE

Thanks for checking in,
but I'm good. Stone tired,
chained to a routine that always ends
before the sun sets.
My feet are still propped on the far armrest
of my dying couch. It creaks, wobbles, splits
at the foggiest images of cleanliness.
My lights are on. All of them.
I called you in tears, but that was months ago.
I've learned lullabies that only I know the words to,
and I will share them with no one,
a steady hymn to rest, its unfulfilling comforts.
I've traded my day-to-day grumblings
for words of encouragement,
promises that all gets better,
that I'm just as fun as I used to be,
though my calendar has emptied itself,
a greyscale map charting surrender,
single point references to times I felt alive.
Each milestone feels like an obituary,
a sad letter stuffed in a bottle,
chucked into a windless sea.
But I'm killing it.
Twelve months, at least twelve more to go.

I REGRET EVERYTHING

Kindness uninhibited
becomes a cruel joke.

We show our hearts
in extreme moments,
rare bouts of vulnerable boldness,

a leap beyond ourselves,
complete surrender,
wrapping our fates around each other's fingers.

There is no greater act of love
than losing composure,
shaking as you open the curtains,
unveil the wreckage meant for no one's eyes but your own.

Allowing me to shine my light
through the mess and cobwebs
as I tell you that nothing is truly empty,
that whatever darkness lurks in your ribcage,
is enough to keep us both alive.

But sacrifice must keep its meaning.
We admire the beauty of fragile minutes,
and then sit alone, let them break us.
No one recovers from this.

ON ENTERING MY GRANDMOTHER'S
HOSPICE ROOM

I started praying in Latin,
a reflex that belongs to someone else.

I counted how many times I've seen her sleeping,
napping the day away
while I pondered the nature of grandmothers.

My happiest memories
grew from the weakened girder
that held her trailer
from the ground.

I miss her old pile of home,
how the window unit hummed
louder than the television.

There was always something good on
and the snack drawer contained
all keys to calm hearts, an early dose
of hiding pain
beneath greedy fingers and refined sugar.

I was afraid to take her hand,
to stir the unwakeable,
her body unconsciously gasping,
her breathing louder than the television.

FIREWORKS

I know we cradled a future,
passed it back and forth,
delicate hands,
one always supporting
its fragile, ethereal head.

We lived in boldface,
the heroes of family newsletters,
what energy youth can bring to old names.

We woke the South,
spoke the names of new towns into existence,
places we'd nest, wooden fences,
lawns large enough to host
the whole church picnic,
Independence Day celebrations just for us.

Held hands and looked into the sky,
blue and red streaks of fire
so vivid they couldn't
have possibly survived themselves.

ON AVOIDANCE FOR THE RIGHT REASONS

I'd confess to something,
but I wouldn't know
whose mannerisms to emulate.
All my heroes have proven themselves
too big, too strong, too imagined,
lovers who've never known
a woman they couldn't convince
to sweat out their tears in silence
and rise only when a forgiving mood
settles in the distance,
begs for green bottles and background music.

Solemnity speaks volumes.
We pride ourselves in blanched escapes,
flashing our biggest fears in public
at mutual friends' weddings,
tracing dancefloors to their widest extremes
just to dodge a single moment's eye contact.
Dismiss all questions with extravagant aplomb.

Congratulations hangs like silly string
after a long night of dancing,
kissing relatives and visiting
some prepaid motel room
we've stocked with sparkling wine,
left half the bed blank
for the best looking option we had
when push finally came
on shove's innocent, preemptively puffed chest.

Do you want to know what follows
the expensive forays into whimsy
and family planning when left
to the sad, graveyard shift think tank?
In spite of all hopes to the contrary,
an imperial voice rises
from the fallen timbers and reminds us:

"history is born to repeat itself."

INTREPID

For Ellen

I could always hear your car before I saw it,
the sharp squeal, metal on metal,
your brake pads long since eroded
beyond their use. You'd lurch
through intersections and beam
through the windshield.

Climbing in, I'd push aside the coffee cups,
water bottles, single-use notions of self-care.
Over the years, you've apologized for more messes
than any one person can make.
It's freeing to let our clutter live
as proof that we were here.

We'd tear out of the parking lot
and unravel the night's plans.
Whatever you want to do, no you,
no, let's just settle for the same
three stops, stay up late complaining
about life and its demands,
the machinery that holds it together,
how some things should just get us
from A to B without expecting
something in return,
how routine maintenance
will be the death of us.

ALPINE LANE

Floodlights and loud voices,
a father tilling the front yard with his own feet.
The sunset stole safety,
left the streets to teem with a million outcomes,
fate's hateful sentries lurking under stop signs,
looking for easy victims.

He never came home on time.
We were leaving our throats on the lawn,
giving up only when tempers out-blushed fear.

He was always off, breaking skateboards
and into parked cars,
rewriting song lyrics in his head,
fueled by fentanyl and a busted compass,
going nowhere in the worst of hurries.

SOUNDLESS TIDINGS

The quiet is hard to reconcile.
It asks too many questions,
unturns stones that would have remained
unseen as long as her voice
hovered above these floorboards.

I'd like to believe she thinks of me.
Once in a while, she turns to tell me something,
reaches for a hand that can't be found,
a phantom limb that forever throbs
in equal bursts of pain and comfort.
I hope against all hopes
that somewhere in this house
is proof that I am more than her absence,
that I was hand-picked by fate,
not just chosen at random.

There's always been a draft here,
a cold that seeps past the window's grip.
Now, it feels personal, sent from a vast distance
to remind me that yesterday
was as good as it's ever going to get,
that if I were worth remembering,
she'd find a way to let me know.

But I try to hold onto her voice,
the last few words she spoke.
The odd, human things that impressed her,
made her stop and gift me her attention,

brief praise, promises
that I am a cut above the rest.

All endings feel personal,
though we make exceptions for our worst fears,
allow them too much control.

Eventually, we let go of tearful musings,
accept the stillness,
the soundless tidings of moving on.

VERMEER WATCHES ME SLEEP

Is this the right kind of ordinary?
Will this room fill the right cups,
wholesome inspiration in powdered dollops,
will it find itself stretched in long, dark fields of oil,
nailed glossy in a white room?

Will people describe me as supple?
This really is how I do it, with my arm
just like this, over my head, irreverent
stakes of artificial light living
as painful pinstripes across my body, my eyes.
I find basketball shorts
to be the most comfortable things to sleep in,
so I adjust my blanket
to cover any logos, as not to confuse
the historian, whistling his tune
of studied grace, only stopping to say things like,
"In his time, to be overweight
was a sign of status, wealth, a wise form of beauty."
Most nights, sleep escapes me.

ON READING AN ENTIRE JASON BALDINGER
BOOK AT A BAR IN ONE SITTING

One shift ends, another begins.
Generous tippers
get free refills, sometimes.

We greet each thistle glass
with warm surprise,
until the sun goes down.

"I should probably eat soon,"
I say a little too late.

Crying in public is like crying alone.
Both make you feel invisible.

CONCERNING APOCALYPSE

Some say the world will end in a Robert Frost poem,
some say in moderation, bit by bit.
I'd wager we never get much further
than the regular, lukewarm destruction,
just lying around when we should be tightening the screws
that keep this carousel turning,
in bed with the wrong people,
the tall tales, tall liars,
a poisoned apple and sleepy sex appeal.
Remember that one guy?
You thought, swore it, it wasn't serious
and then you were crying,
calling from a stairwell?
That's where it'll all go down.
The world will burn
while you come to your senses
on the cold, dirty floor. And we'll curse
the tile of all things, we'll say we called it,
saw it coming from a mile away
and retreated into our blankets.
Just got comfy with our habits,
just let them take right over.

IN WHICH JERA IS JUST TRYING TO LIVE
HER LIFE, AND I CONSIDER REACHING OUT
MULTIPLE TIMES, BUT DON'T WANT TO BE
THAT GUY

The empty chat box,
the cursor daring me to light a conversation

in the middle of the night.
I try rubbing two thoughts together

and retire into the cold night
with nothing to cover up with

except my lonely inclinations
and lack of imagination.

"If it seems," I whisper,
blowing geysers of whiskey breath

into the frosty air, "If it seems
like I only talk when it's convenient,

it's because I never got used to bothering you
and feel as if I shouldn't start now."

THE BAFFLED KING

For Leonard Cohen...and David, I guess

Compose hallelujah.
Try it. Take a pen and put it to paper,
watch the hallelujah
grow into some recognizable shape.

Now that you've failed,
compose an apology. Five or so couplets
that can cast your hubris as imagery,
a picture of you giving up, frustrated.
Crumpling paper as each attempt
sounds less and less like hallelujah.

Apologies are weak
as long as they're just words,
so go outside, take to the streets.
Talk to the first five people you see.

Make their lives easier,
mow their lawns, help their mothers
move into their last home.
Give them twenty dollars,
so they cannot feel guilty
for eating out tonight.
Put an arm around their shoulder,
tell them it's okay
to have to apologize for things.

Now that you've made their problems your problems,
go home and apologize. In the mirror.
Who the hell are you
to give mercy? To decide
who needs it?

Feel lost. Pace. Walk your floor,
the same path in your carpet over and over
until you actually are lost. Baffled. Until every breath
you draw
is an apology.

Now tie yourself to your chair
and remember that writers who deal in secrets
die unread. You will try again.

Compose an apology
in pencil. Proofread, erasing every appearance
of "you made me feel"

and replacing it with
with forgiveness,
with a nod and a wink,
with hallelujah.

MOTHER'S DAY IN TEXAS

For Hilary

Brushing the knots from your mother's hair
as she talks about the new order of things,
how no one has the time to be helpful,
or the patience to take things apart,
put them in their proper place.

HOW DID IT FEEL WHEN YOU DELETED
OUR PHOTO OFF OF YOUR INSTAGRAM?

We don't carry baggage, we carry lassos
and the time has come to move on,
rope someone else with our feelings,
drag their nights behind our galloping will and
hope they survive the long, painful cut through the mud.
It's not that I mind the gesture.
It's hard to sever ties, so we might as well start
by trimming the fat before we remove the heart entirely.
It's just a picture. Two people smiling about something,
with a filter that made us look like sepia gods,
soaked in the sun of a beautiful, infinite day.
But I can't stop thinking about the morning of.
We stopped for breakfast and you told me,
in between bites of your McGriddle,
that thing I promised I'd never repeat,
I reciprocated and we cried,
guiding our horses for another round
of circling the barrels long-since filled
with poison from our respective upbringings.
But we drove and eventually, we parked.
We found the sun and shed the greater weight
for the smaller moment.
For company so perfect
we had to save it. Smile into your camera
and preserve the day. Celebrate.
Not because we found happiness,
but because we'd found each other.
But fuck me, I guess.

EDDIE BLAMES TIKTOK FOR EVERYTHING

This generation invented the short attention span. In
my day, we pricked the ends of our fingers with folding
knives, used the blood to diagram sentences, and let
the red shine through, remind us that everything we
wrote was wrong. We were ungrateful, didn't bow
low enough when our fathers spoke, didn't whisper
quietly enough, checked out bibles with a card catalog,
wrote confessions in cursive, hit the aisles with a
shotty memory and a magnifying glass. Books never
collected dust, because we used them to prop open
doors to opportunity. Encyclopedic idols of nine-to-
five humility and sweaty reverence. And at night you
could hear our grandfathers crying, because even they
had it easier, never had to haul the wagon with a leather
strap fixed to their teeth, not like their forebears, not
like it used to be. This generation invented groupthink,
invented dancing in spite of the world and its
unwillingness to provide music. They invented doing
things the way they want. And didn't you see? There's
proof now, something in the water, scientists have
identified the magnetic stream that flows straight from
their phones to the part of their brain that crumbles at
the thought of work. I saw it, read the article, you can
find it on Facebook.

GRIEF II

for Rebecca

Arrived at the pool hall

with more on my mind
than I could ever bear to say out loud.
I could have stayed home,
finessed a little more mileage from my sofa,
lathered my evening in comfortable wishes
and let the night dredge up hope
in its usual way.

About this time, it would have dried,
the sagging spine of my couch reminding me
that I hate it here, that good times
don't grow on their own.

I've been told I focus too much on the past,
but I don't think I'm even remembering it correctly.
Our best years forgotten,
it feels like we were blindfolded,
let loose to play pin-the-memory on our heroes.

Snatched them off to find ourselves alone.
No voice to guide us up and off
our skinned knees. No one to ward off
the sleepless nights we will inherit,
or the pacts we form to escape them.
Just scrambled images
glued together by hearsay.

If only our habits tasted
as good as we remember,
if the people we miss could resurface,
hold us up with both hands,
promise us that we are right where we are supposed to be,

that home is just a four-letter word,
that real friends will come along, share the weight,
that offerings are as big as their intentions,
that pool tables have the same number of legs as the
one in your kitchen,

but they can hold so much more.

GIRL WITH A PEARL EARRING BY
JOHANNES VERMEER

Fell in love with a woman once
who mispronounced the names of cities
she claimed she'd been to, wore stones plucked
from the mouths of plastic mollusks.

Swore up and down that the warmth
beneath her sheets held the secrets
that bind our joy to the Earth. I always
imagined she was a good kisser.

Wore scarves her aunt left her,
from when chemo started popping up
at holidays, in any conversation with mom,
every dinner, told her stories

about life and its limitlessness,
its utter lack of limits.
She's married, now.
Iowa, I think.

MY ZAFU IS COLLECTING DUST

I brought a few prayers
and let them sit on the hardwood floor,
blew lightly, tried to get the kindling to catch.

They say if you breathe
your heartbeat will relax
to the proper cadence,
the rhythm of god,
precursor to all gentle paces.

I don't know if it works that way,
but I sleep easier
when I invite death. It comes,
takes my plans
to some ridiculous grave,
a cold hole where self-importance
will hopefully shrivel in peace.

I rarely make the time,
and I hope it's a one-way street,
that there's not a heart somewhere,
waiting for our breath
to set a calmer beat.

ON APOLOGIZING FOR MY OWN EXISTENCE

They say we live on borrowed time,
but I don't know where to return it.
I need reminders that the space I inhabit
can belong to me as long as I am in it.

Yes, you've said it before,
but I'd rather you beat a dead horse
than a live one,
rather you tell me it's in my head
than become the monster inside it,
the one who feeds on the timid,
demands its precious time back.

IN HAYS, AMERICA ON A THURSDAY

for Anja

I'm ordering another,
discussing denim at great length,
everything it has to say about form,
curves contained by ardorous thread
and cut-off audacity.
 I feel full -- beer has always been
my worst idea -- but regret
is just a catchall, a word we think
we are supposed to use,
though pain often comes
with angelic rewards,
like a few moments
with this night's brightest star
hanging under the ninth sign,
slumming it in Western Kansas,
talking about sage bundles
and organic independence.
 I wish we could light this place up,
cull good vibes from the fumes,
clear the air of every last
troublesome thought,
leave us with nothing
but the smell of singed herbs,
chilled glasses,
and a promise
to not say anything too weird.

HAVE YOU EVER SEEN A SUNSET?

I don't mind saying that there are no sunsets
like Kansas sunsets, so much open space,
flat ground to fall to,
all knees and dropped jaws
at the pink, red slit in the sky.
Last time I was in New York,
a woman asked me if I had ever had a bagel
before and I wish we had that kind of arrogance.
That we were members of an elite
breakfast pastry society,
the only ones to have ever tasted
the things we hold dear.
And maybe arrogance isn't the right word.
She was probably trying to be nice, offering
a small slice of what brings her to the ground,
so from now on, whenever I make introductions,
I'll just ask, "Have you ever seen a sunset?"

RIVERTOWNE

Picked my brother up from jail,
drove his ass south so he could cry in a Wal-mart,
slick-eyed wonder at the people,
the clothes hanging in every direction,
enough space to reach out his arms
and say "I know what I want for dinner."
He doesn't sleep, he paces across the hotel room,
chugging complimentary coffee
and mumbling future plans,
making them up as he goes.

Tomorrow, his life starts fresh.
As long as I'm willing to drive him
as far from home as possible.
They can heal anyone down in Arkansas,
dip their heels in Lake Dardanelle,
immortality restored.
It worked for me, too.
On the way back,
one small stop off I-40,
God's purest work:
spare ribs
and the best potato salad I've ever eaten.

ON FORGIVENESS AS A DELAYED
APPOINTMENT

I have named injuries
That are irreconcilable
Unable to be bandaged by mere time
Our best efforts at doing better

Thumbtacks hold it all together
Maps and calendars
Home decor for those who are never actually at home
They're going places, keeping appointments
Toasting each entry
Having the difficult conversations
The rest of us put off

My brother never understood
Proper time and place
Couldn't keep appointments
Can't apologize from the confines
Of his plastic urn

AGGIEVILLE

I was with my friend who died a few Aprils ago.
Took a break to escape the basement fumes
and breathe in the spring.
He met a woman dancing on the sidewalk,
hollering into the fresh evening,
doing the things people like to roll their eyes at,
as if we've never just tried to enjoy ourselves.

The pieces came together, he shook the charm
from his curly hair and before I knew it
the two of them were haunting corners,
backs against the walls,
sneaking into the alley
to shed decorum and feed as strays.

Who am I to get involved?
Except I knew too much. I've seen him angry.
I shivered at the thought, what the cocktail of booze
and the long-time-coming kind of sex would be like,
so I betrayed him, whispered to her companion,
"Hey, I think your friend is trying to leave with mine."

A good night had slipped from his grip
and he never knew it was my fault.
He whined about it for a few days
until the bruises along the seams of his ego
healed over, got their color back.
But guilt is a stupid thing,
and I've been thinking about it a lot lately,

the things he said about frustration,
fitful sleep, the kind of shame that burns in your balls,
makes you feel a foot shorter.

I think about the rails and countertops we've leaned on,
the spaces we've shared and made light in,
the people we've absorbed into our Aggieville antics,
and it starts to feel like a bigger and bigger picture,
but then I realize that neither the woman nor her friend
knows he's dead.

COLUMBUS

We both lived in the same town at different times, and
wouldn't you know it, we still walk around with the
same favorites, the same restaurants, the same blue
plates hovering over our tongues like holy question
marks. Remember Ruth Anne's? Fresh catfish? And
how the word tea used to mean something? How a
certified, real Coca-Cola hits different in the Georgia
summer and man, it would have been great if we could
have shared a plate of frog legs, fried squirrel ten years
earlier, back when we were still whistling to the future
we built in our heads, still seeing the forest for the meat
crawling in the trees.

A1A

No one's ever come home from Satellite Beach
without bruised heels
and a neck that could blush
a lobster into shame.

They got so much coquina rock
submerged in the sand,
there's almost no room to trip.
But we always find a way.

Broken toenails, forgotten bait buckets
left dotted up and down
Florida's Eastern coast.

THE MONDRIAN COLLECTION BY
YVES SAINT LAUREN

god!!!!!! sloped shoulders, and the flat stomachs
of 1966
let's play hopscotch, let the eyes, exuberantly double dutch
and scream. we've seen the end, the pinnacle of physical
fluency
we won

IOWA WORKSHOP MODEL

No, I don't want to talk
about eye opening adjectives, about craft.
I want to tell you what it's like
to drown
in front of everyone.
And how if you scream and fight
fifty feet below the surface
of your own shortcomings
it just looks like you're dancing.
The thing is,
we sculpt our stories into songs
and pretend we are elevating language
by calling our red blood crimson
and praising each sunrise
as god's newest beginning,
by thatching nets out of our hang-ups
and dragging them along the bottom
of our most recent memories.
We inject humor because we know
our families will laugh
and let our cries for help
hover just beyond their attention span.
We use imagery to hide
how window-streaked and grimy
our perspectives really are.
Maybe, we'd be better off
recanting our embarrassments
to a professional,
instead of this circle. Storyteller's

are liars by nature, absorbing each other's pain
just to wring out their bodies, let it all drip
into crudely formed stanzas with their name
neatly tucked under the title.
For once, let's just say what we mean.
Spend more time on healing,
less time sweating
over line breaks.

MAYBE WE SHOULD START A POET'S BOWLING LEAGUE

For John Dorsey

Would we play against other poets?
The New York School in their mismatched jackets,
violently sending the ball away.
Short, choppy movements
in any direction they feel like.

Or a dapper group of modernists
who never take their turn.
They're too busy writing anthems
about the polished floors
about the sine wave skyline of the pins,
how coquina rock and strip mall architecture
gives them hope.

Or other kinds of writers?
The tough-guy pulp fiends
who shine their bowling balls with ink ribbons.
Or worse, Bret Easton Ellis
who spends the night not bowling at all.
Refusing to pay the price for the shoe rental.
Just tells us we're all doing it wrong.
He'd teach us the right way,
but there are simply too many rules
for our Miller High Life minds.

But we know who it would really be.
And they would win.

A patchwork of men with custom bags.
"Hank" embroidered in the center.
They don't come for the cheese fries and beer,
but for the taste of competition.
Majored in marketing and now look at the bowling alley
and see only its output potential,
the ratio of pitchers being served
to waitresses being paid to peddle them.
And a few others who are surprised to see
that poets can lift bowling balls at all.
They thought books were for the weak.
The only legs they have to stand on.

UPON DISCOVERING THE INTERROBANG

I've long since mastered the art
of feigning surprise. My pen gasps,
shouts in the same tired way as everyone else's.
But once, someone had the nerve
to dream, to form beauty out of the aether,
to leave our curveless hearts to stand in shock.

I've written plenty,
but I've never had that courage,
or such a talent for naming things.

YOU HAVE THE BEST STORIES

Courage as a coping skill.
Jovial quests into caprice
and its equivocal nothingness,
just abandoned parking lots, long-lashed jungles
of low-rent fame and murky consequences.

Legends live on. Second-hand stories
rehashed at parties
while their players dry out
on a half-sunken sofa.

Long evenings, lonely dinners,
the same show always playing in the background.

ODE TO A ROMANCE NOVEL

I used to hide the cover, as public eyes
like to eat the things you love,
but no one should be shaming buoyancy,
the celebration of impossible luck.
Which of course, they do, they all do,
after asking, "Has love become passe?"
If the cover were reversed,
or if the woman died alone, having loved
only to feel left, or if the hulking, kilted man
were slim and only cared for himself, his appetites,
would its cover be blessed with a medal?
Miserable Ever After has won enough PEN awards,
don't you think?

APHRODITE SYNDROME

We've all had at least one day
where we made our children
carry the weight of our anger,
haul it straight into the ocean
and dare them not to venture out too far.

But from the sea foam comes new life
and trading past mistakes for possibility
is a task noble enough for a goddess.

She wants more than memory,
the mere shape of a father, kept whole,
who shouldn't have had to die
for her to become herself.

ADONIS 2.0

I'm afraid she uses me to fill a void,
a nagging echo
that won't settle on its own.

I dare not ask how I compare,
the silhouette I stepped through,
the towering figure I'm standing in for.

Pouting, I start to push the issue,
sure that I leave no shape at all.
I want to be a strand
of colorful thread woven into her tapestries,
some small part of her story
that holds the bigger picture together.

But I let pride wane,
accept simple facts.
I'm no more than the doubts that haunt me.
But lately, life's blows have been softened,
the beasts outside my house
are howling a little less loudly.
I've been feeling more certain
I live up to my own name.

PASTIMES

What if the things I love about football
are the things you hate about your parents?
The volume, the rough and tumble
soundbites that hang as salty humor,
wishes brewed solely in tribal fear. What if
we named our limitations
instead of carting them around in the dark?
Blanket lies about distance,
that the only thing stopping us
from strapping on our neatly molded violence,
painting our faces with crude black bars,
is the railing. Metal and concrete:
tidewater symbols that bear no meaning,
need no explanation.

JUDGMENTAL WALLS

Tempranillo, sour-lipped
a song resting on my tongue,
but it just can't find the
air. I want to sing perfect
Spanish, but I've only had the app
for two weeks, and no bards
ever found favor with *Yo
quiero una hamburguesa.*

So I talk, bouncing my wine-
soaked voice off the judgmental
walls of my apartment and shiver
at how thin it sounds.

I puff my chest like Lord Byron,
and say things Lord Byron would say,
keeping my eyes averted
from the mirror.

FOR LOVE, NOT NOTORIETY

I (too) have no patience
for the masculine romp
of Hemingway's Havana blues,

chewing up the band and bar
as he tries to "dance."

Nor is drinking
the most interesting thing about me.

But the glasses I leave stacked
to glow

in the router's indicator lights,
around my computer tower

are no less heartwarming
than the absence of Van Gogh's ear.

Poets are lovers, and my tongue
is addicted to love,

to carrying the caramel, peat,
smoke, sour mash
and cursing the weight.

"Anabell Lee,"
the poet said. "Laura,"
the poet said, but "double Dickel on the rocks,"
and suddenly love is a joke.

HEMINGWAY TAKES ME FISHING

A harpoon in one hand,
rum in the other.
A sea so calm,
he has to invent a tempest:
vague threats, worn-out tall tales
of cabin fever, murderers at high sea.
He gets angry that I'm not nervous,
as if he'd travel back alone
without anyone to hear
his tales of sweaty heroism.
I'm over old-man bravado
and its extended metaphors
about the threat of nameless death,
an inability to rise with the tide.

JACK LONDON WOULD HATE YOU

You're fresh air adjacent at best.
We see your shoulders drop
in practiced relaxation,
taking in a world you'll never appreciate.
That smell is your own sunscreen,
propane cooking fires.

GRAB YOUR NOTEBOOK

For Skyler

For at least ten minutes,
let's ditch this 8 to 5 tether
holding us to our chairs
and see if we can will the goalposts closer,
emerge in the current outside these walls,
that carries others
to their declared notions of success.

We'd do it, too if we had the time,
money, courage to bet on our best efforts.
If we didn't have granters writing our bios,
sentencing us to non-profit obscurity.

Forget the meeting, let's make a list:
the top five celebrities and sports cars
we'll take with us to the top,
to the bestseller shelf,
to neighboring houses with connected backyards
where our better halves are waiting for us,
cold drinks in hand, dinner on the grill.

The word "congratulations"
forever dripping from their lips.

OPEN LETTER TO WINY MAAS AND THE
RESIDENTS OF THE DOUBLE HOUSE

I am programmed for noise, but too often find myself
silently baiting the patinated habits of two weeks ago.
I wish I could leave this room and find a new one, a
hallway that could spin me on my heels and send me
back. My bed is made, all fabric is fresh now, my family is
waiting outside, there's a party downstairs where no one
gossips and we all cry joyous tears at the smell of melted
cheese. Mostly, I just wish that I couldn't see, hear,
feel my neighbors through my window, that whoever
built this crumbling rental would come and explain
themselves, tell me it was a sense of humor that invented
loneliness, not some mosquito-like need to move from
body to body.

IN WHICH JERA TAKES THE ROLE OF
ELIZABETH BENNET AND MR. DARCY
WRITES HIS APOLOGETIC LETTER TO HER

I have shown the weaker sinews
of my character. A weakness
not worthy of this letter,
of your precious time.
And while I see cause to step down,
let your heart soar unencumbered
by my selfish crusade, I am emboldened.
I find my heart raked,
left shredded by these delicate hands,
your hands, Elizabeth, hold my entire future.
You may ask why you above all else,
why one picks just one flower
out of the whole field,
but it's a much more obvious choice than you think.

The world is a dull, dreary place, and even
sunflowers look brown and faded
under the right course
of cloudy shadows and disposition.
But there you were, sunny charisma in hand,
like a powder charge in a prairie,
I could see no other if I tried.

Stop pretending you're as invisible
as Mary, my heart is not so lazy.
And stop fearing you'll become
as frivolous as Lydia if you just let your heart
accept what it deserves for once.

Not even Jane could look that graceful
in a leather jacket. Those boots
fit to traverse the hearts
of a thousand gentlemen
much more worthy of your esteem.

If you can summon any feelings for me at all,
guide them toward forgiveness,
and see me as the man who sees you
as you ought to be seen, make known
your heart and I will wait as long as it takes,
and say I'm sorry as many times as you'd like.

OETR

Can't tell if it's the mucinex
or my hangover talking,

but I'm glad you're laughing.
I'm trying to build a single thought

from absent pieces,
elusive crumbs fallen from old dictionaries

as you insist that small words
are much bigger than their parts.

My brain and its sister nerves
are sentenced, marched to the gallows.

No final words,
just heavy eyes

and a bloodshot thirst
for the obvious.

SPLASH

You said it was my cologne, as you peeled yourself like an orange, leaving a trail of bright scraps through my apartment.

I don't wear any, but now I'm in love, at least with the part of you that gives yourself to the scent of Paul Masson on my breath and maybe the little I spilled on my shirt.

ADVENTUROUS

The kind of people that love erratic weather
'cause they think it's their reflection:
I am such a Tempest,
a heavy blanket of ice,
but I'll melt by noon tomorrow.
Or quake when they read Kerouac:
I am such a seed in the wind,
riding the current, landing
wherever fortune will have me,
Then, off I go again.
People only say these things
at the lamest parties,
ones they've obviously been to
before, holding a beer that
doesn't taste too much like beer,
wearing a shirt that says Bahamas
Carnival Cruise 2002.

OBITUARY

I'm all about grace and seeing the very best
sparkle through our nastiest moments,
but I gotta admit, some of those times
I saw it was you calling and dunked my phone
into the surreptitious folds of my pocket.
To be fair, I always intended
to make it right, call you back
when I could handle it, equipped with
golden excuses and smooth segues
to get to the center of whatever you wanted
to talk about. It's just that lately
negativity keeps capturing the few bastions
I have left, so I'm taking ownership,
setting boundaries marked with denim,
cowardice, and holistic intentions.
I'm doing what's good for me for once,
but I'll call you back, we'll catch up soon,
soon, we'll hash all this out.

HANNAH'S PARENTS' HOUSE

One day, we'll stop by unannounced,
silently greet the statue of Mary
in their front lawn. Admire
the flower beds.

Stifle our chuckles as we knock
and greet Dawn and Steve.
By then, their faces will erupt, all smiles,
the expressive fireworks of a pleasant surprise.
We'll be guided in as we answer their questions,
laugh at our own hijinks.
Tell them what we've been up to.
Leave out about half of it.

Make jokes about the Vikings,
take over their couch,
turn on their TV
and count the times we all laugh in unison.

If we're lucky,
she'll have a whole pyrex dish
full of chicken and noodles in her freezer.
She had it ready. She knew this day would come.

Nothing warms my heart more
than the defeat of egg noodles
by my teeth,
the smell of pepper and chicken fat,
this house.

Of course, we wish Hannah could be here,
but then our visit would lack audacity. And besides,
she can have chicken and noodles
whenever she wants.

SOMEWHERE AROUND ALVA

For Tyler

We were all coffee and carnage,
joking about how terrible it would be
if we flew off the road
and breathed our last in a damp ditch.
Not for the obvious,
but because "what could be worse
than dying in Oklahoma?"

The last time we stopped for food
we had to stop again for Tums
to soothe the fire in our antsy guts.
We declared we'd never
eat gas station pizza again,
but here we are touting coffee
and greasy food, heroic levels
of assumed invincibility. I'm just saying,
maybe we should master living
before we talk shit on death.

SHE LIKES ME SOBER, I GUESS

The life of the party
has moved on, found its lifeblood
in habits more interesting
than the contents of a liquor cabinet.

But drinking will always be my first idea,
even if it can barely be heard
over the present moment
and its steady hum of balance.

I offer to run to the store,
to fill my van with wine
and pour us both into oblivion,
dredge the night of its last few honorable plans,
just toasting her arrival and inevitable exit
in equal gulps of red pleasure.

But she prefers a slow burn,
a passion that keeps itself lit,
never casts a flame
bigger than its shadow,
than its ability to remember
why it ever reached for a corkscrew.

CINCINNATI

Let's pretend this is the street corner,
the one where we met, chipped paint
and a familiar bustle, no,
the one where we first saw each other,
passed by with warm shivers of interest,
heads turning to smile at a long life.

Over here, right off campus is where
I paid for an overly steamed cortado
and decided who I'd become,
a big name to haunt neatly sorted spines
in our favorite bookstore.

It's been awhile since we ambled near
the old neighborhood, its ashcan lore
still fresh on my mind.

Chocolate, chili,
where did we get the best milkshakes?
Can we go for a drive?
All I ask is that you smile when you see me,
remember all the other cities
we've yet to visit,
all the landmarks we wished we'd built.

THIRTIES

All this talk about worldview,
about where do you get your courage from
to get up each day, to shave once in a while.
Jesus never really had to do his thirties, though.
We all just want to know
why and who we will become,
to nail our hands to it, having carried it
for everyone to see and they sing,
it is right and just.
The whole time, he had an idea,
someone filling his jugs,
changing them from bravado to wine
and he was actually doing it,
he was actually doing it.

CLASSIC NEW YORK CITY BALLET

There is a correct way to discuss classical music,
but I haven't figured it out yet.

In the minds of my fellow Southeast Kansans,
it appears to be only in a tux,
with a urine-hued champagne and the whole world
resting in my hand.

They've never listened,
and have obviously never had champagne,
but I get their point.

And when I do happen upon a hideout,
a hovel of like-minded Offenbach-ophiles,
the furniture is most vertically unwelcoming,
their brows quizzically furrowed
as they chew on my mispronunciation
of Boccherini's name.

Ever incapable of balancing that scale
between pretentious
and whatever the opposite of pretentious is,
I listen on.

And when asked what is coursing through my headphones,
I've been known to fib
so as to avoid any misunderstanding entirely.

But I remember sweating at Lincoln center,
the New York City Ballet balcony in May,
being assaulted by the Manhattan humidity,
swirling some knock-off champagne and a few bars I'd
just heard on my tongue.

While I've yet to perfect how to discuss classical music,
that night, I mastered its enjoyment,
crying alone to Mozartiana in an obstructed-view seat,
drinking at every intermission,
and planning things to say about the weather.

I've seen a million movies about New York,
and none of them have characters who sweat.

TRULY, I'D PUNCH NINETEEN-YEAR-OLD ME RIGHT IN THE FACE

For Dan Wright

Dan is sick of people
hiding behind almost.
Their intentions weighing up
to a verifiable, though long-winded, zero.
Me? I'm tired of "used to"
and the promises to start up again.

"I used to play in a band."
"I used to eat better."
As if any splinter of our old selves
would have a clue
what we're supposed to do next.

It's not like we'd listen to them, anyway.

OXYGEN

A throb behind the eyes, a tense elbow. I greet
indecision with paralysis, an afternoon spent sinking.
I don't know if one chooses to unplug themselves.
Perhaps, the numbness chooses you, believe me, there's
a longing for old textures, new colors. And I have no
shortage of places I'd rather be, fires I'd rather be igniting.
I want to boil, write love songs to Laura Dern and
know what it feels like to drive a convertible. I want to
beg for my life instead of watch it slowly percolate into
a dark, wet mess. But only if it ends up being worth it,
if the night ends with PBR and neon tombstones, if
there's someone blonde who'd trade a life's worth of
joy if it promises survival.

GEORGIA

Two, oozy red beers deep
and heaven's guide-on greets me again,
brings me chili fries and a playful purse of the lips.
I am not an idiot and I'm not even shopping,
but tell that to my pen
'cause I'm writing an opera on my ticket,
a love song for four voices
and a chorale composed entirely in numerals,
a big enough tip to pay for her tuition.

THE GORGEOUS BASS PRO SHOP
EMPLOYEE WHO DENIED MY CREDIT CARD
APPLICATION AND GAVE ME TWO FREE HATS

First, I'm sorry for noticing.
Failure will do that to you,
heighten your worst senses
to generate a more accurate picture,
the perfect snapshot of rejection.
Second, it pains me
to see myself how you must see me.
Barely a man, with an awkard smile
a credit score that feeds
with the pleco.
Forego the scripted congeniality,
the promise of more explanation in the mail.
Just kill me now, and set me up
with the stuffed fauna,
or set me free.
Click yes, click print,
and guide me to the sleeping bags
suited for all temperatures.
For what it's worth,
I would have used this money for good.
Real adventures, oiled with bear grease
and charted on antique maps.
While I can't stake the voyage on my own,
thanks for the few moments of your time,
for your warmth, for the free hats.

PRETTY AND NICE

She was the ultimate example
of a woman who is pretty and nice
to you — which never happens —
and so you think you're in love, suddenly
dropping dead birds at her feet and she's like
What the hell are you doing?
And you try to pretend
you're fluent in human, as if
all relationships aren't burdensome
messes, just chances to flex your
what-the-hell-are-you-doing muscles.

OVERTHINKING

I actually love Magritte so much,
I've found myself browsing Amazon,
pricing bowler hats, preparing
justifications: "Oh this old thing?"
"It was a gag gift --
funny, right?" Anything other than
I thought it was cool, thought
it would make me a tad more interesting.

But I won't do it, 'cause I don't want to wear
the coolest hat, for innocent self-esteem reasons,
and get mistaken
for the coffee-shop soul-patch dragons,
the beasts breathing "friend-zone"
in non-filtered plumes of smoke.

But somewhere,
trying and not trying become
two heads of the same whatever,
a double-bladed cliche that
makes you feel like you're wearing
a dumb hat and everyone's pointing,
especially when you hear it
from one of those "friend-zone" guys.

IN WHICH JERA MAKES ME REASSESS
MY LIFE CHOICES

Not gonna lie, it's gotten easy to just shrug the genetic
evidence off my shoulders, to feed the emotional meter
with bottle caps and shots of cheap rum.

Advice can come from medical professionals or the same
tired friends, and it's so easy, so easy to just say "here for a
good time, not a long time," because it always feels a little
like a dare. They say, "If you don't stop, you'll pulverize
your liver, make your blood sugar do jumping jacks as you
lay on the floor and succumb to your final toast." And it's
like they all wanna see it, so we buckle up and repeat our
old procedures for feeling something new.

But the other day, coming from you, it stung a little.

THE WEEK BEFORE I GOT SOBER...
THE FIRST TIME

"I am growing up, no more poems
about cigarettes and wine."
I pour a glass of wine.

I need at least two before my throat
wises up, remembers that the
acrid taste of a menthol
is almost certainly followed
by a humming joy, flashbacks to its youth.

I light a cigarette and remember
what Tony Hoagland told me.
It takes me too long to realize
he's never told me anything.

Maybe, it's how we read,
the way we tie cords to the strains of beauty
so we can find our way home.
Makes us feel as if we've made a friend
every time we visit the local bookstore.

It all unravels. I go down the list:
the poets I haven't crossed paths with,
the fathers we suddenly don't have in common,
the tundrous nights they didn't get me through.
It was just me, a blanket,
an unrequited call for help.

Caring is a choice
sometimes and I guess I have to decide.
I start coughing, blaming the cold
hanging onto the end of October
for the sharp stab in my lungs,
the subtle smear of tears
across my eyes, like two sallow
reflecting pools in a courtyard
no one has ever visited.

I flick my cigarette into the grass
and regret my lack of foresight.
I regret my impulsive leaps into the night,
the way my knees feel when I fall,
my lack of interesting things to write about.

MINISTERING AT MILLER'S PUB

A mendicant voice, gruff and weary
Preaching devotion for the local stuff
Beer seasoned with team pride
And hop varietals that sound fake
Dredged in the essence of pineapple
Or some shit, but nevertheless comes chilled
And rolls in at a solid 8.5 ABV

I'll take it, I want it
And it pairs well with the fish and chips
The Italian beef, the calamari
Or my tastebuds have been left
To wander the loop
As I toast the overpriced quarry
And the bowtied server
Who let me sample every beer on the menu

There is love here
And it deserves to be noticed
To be recommended to anyone
Who sits near me, to be etched
In the bathroom stalls
Though I've never been able to get the horizontal cuts
To show as anything more
Than a near invisible line

ON SOBRIETY

I grieve for my shadow,
how historically its formless husk
was towed to die in dimly lit hovels,
the wanton caves of the sleepless.

Or tossed
into barroom corners while its master
conducted his ritual business,
sacrifices offered in pints of blood,
would reap no reward, no cosmic attention.

If shadows had ears,
he could've recognized a higher voice,
telling everyone to go home,
that this altar is no place to linger.
It was built from rotten wood and bad advice.

If shadows could speak,
he would've begged for death, an end to his misery,
to cut the progeny loose,
and let hard work glimmer
in the sun.

BARGAINING WITH BAD LUCK

We use the same few tricks
to get from place to place.
On the way up, but tethered
to some pretty dirty habits,
icebreakers about our dreams,
about karaoke and hair gel,
how the volume is just grating in here.
And did you know your eyes
are as blue as the silicone trim
on my phone case? That if you hold
your ear to my ear, you can hear
the subtle waves of a polluted, brown ocean?
Let's talk about our exes,
their punishing past chained to our ankles,
even though they're on their backs,
their legs fully extended in a toast
to what we could have been.
Let's talk until a bruised and buzzed
hope foams at the surface, gets the light
to change shade just a little,
just enough to turn our envy into
lime juice. I love it when a night
ends way better than it started.

SCENES OF EVERYDAY LIFE

Fine, simp for the Romans and their quest for heaven on
Earth, history that smacks the spectator in seven dolorous
strokes.

But have you ever just sighed before? The kind that
cleaves corset strings, balloons the chest then gorges out
of satisfaction, faith alone, a job most certainly well done.

A perfect smear of peanut butter, an improved clinch knot
set perfectly, seven brilliant nylon fingers snug against
the hook, a nothing-but-net kind of relief, a bean bag
flung cleanly through the hole in the ramp that backyard
summer evening, a child, pink and well dressed, looking
just like your wife two seconds before it dribbles pudding,
chocolate smears on the lace and satin, those are ideal
moments. Ones who've held eternity by its cracked spine,
moments that most certainly died because of and for our
sins.

LISTENING TO SKIP JAMES

My only memories of Mississippi are a Biloxi motel
and a spot of woods in Hattiesburg
where a woman I call freckles
undressed in front if me
for the third time.
But I've been crying
to the Bentonia school
since I was fifteen, learning new names
to call the devil.
Why is heartache always the woman's fault?
I didn't ask. Not until it was too late,
not until I had squandered my high school years
filling composition notebooks
with the top ten things I hate about myself.
Or was it the top ten reasons I was alone?
Projecting has always come naturally.

TO CARLO AND THE POPE

Unlocked doors mark an invitation
to the black-haired poet
who bums life off his friends
and sings their stories as if they mattered.
He will leave, drift
with a sudden toss of his scarf
and a cocked eyebrow goodbye.

Out there also,
a hooded do-gooder wanders,
seeking love, but finding a cost.
His arguments of Hell,
here or elsewhere,
reek of ash and taste bitter,
leaving electric streaks
on the sides of my tongue.
But at least, he means them.

I have hated them both
and I have studied there,
in the streets and in the cathedrals,
I have watched the towns die at night,
slowly and surely, collapsed and snoring.
The moon side-eyed my walk home
with a panic that laughs itself quiet.
I feared for the entire Midwest
and thought it might never wake again.
Heavy doctrine curled in Atlas strife,
but my spine, like Carlo's is fickle.

One truth is clear:
hell is a place where the bars close before midnight.

FRISCO BURGER

for Jason Ryberg

Not all leaps of faith are so rewarding,
they don't all come with cheese.
But expectation is getting easy to defeat
in this land of wandering children,
of cellphone signal so faint
it's crushed under the slightest hint of urgency.
And frankly, I prefer not to be asked
how I like my burgers cooked.
You either know there's only one right answer,
or you wouldn't be able to deliver
my version of pink in the middle anyway.
Historically, perspective has been shaped
by fuel far worse than silence, griddle grease,
a stomach spoiled by its own sensitivities.
We should all take leaps of faith more often.

IN WHICH JERA GETS MARRIED

The balcony holds us to glow
in the spring's best volley of sunlight.
My whole body is warm,
my soul is a furnace. Pulled pork,
the Wichita air, your white dress,
and Tyler's best impression
of me at any given moment
are working like coals,
keeping my spirits chugging,
enjoying my fifth or ninth glass of cab-sav,
occasionally peering at the river,
watching the water carry these moments downtown.

I'm not dancing at your wedding
because joy has found its match.
There is no enemy
my self-consciousness cannot kill.
But I agree with Orlando.
We need to find the right words,
something that can tell you
how truly happy we are
to see one of our own shining
in the sparks of her own making,
a beautiful summer wedding
where all eyes are on you
and you deserve every minute of it.
But actions speak louder than words,
even when shouted from the blacktop
after the reception, even when they're carved

from our purest faults. So we talk
in gesture, in our habits.
Let's just say we toasted you
and only you five,
or nine, or sixteen times.

I'M NOT AFRAID OF DYING ALONE, I'M AFRAID OF DYING IN FRONT OF EVERYONE

"I would spend the rest of my life turning to speak to you."
-Don Delillo

There are some things you get over,
others you climb inside, making yourself
comfortable, resting in its bitter glow.

I can't decide if I want closure:
fifteen minutes of tears
and an apology I can mount on my wall,

or to meet up, pretend
separation is always temporary,
and here are fifteen old jokes to prove it.

You hated my green beanie,
and I haven't worn it since you left.
Maybe small acts of kindness
can raise the dead.

Are all centipedes venomous?
Or just the ones in the movies you like?
You know, the dark evenings
we'd laze through as we peeled sensibility
clean off our backs.

I will always crawl back to you,
but the window is open,
and my eyes are closed,
and here I go, picking up speed.

THE WAY SHE LOOKS AT YOU

You can't tell if it's pity or lust,
but it's dripping on your carpet,
and you haven't the energy for another mess.
Grab her hands, swallow her whispers,
let the dusk do its thing.

COLLECTOR'S EDITION

Prayed in the stacks of a university library
for divine favor wrought with ambition
and was charged a fee: a dollar
for every time I didn't follow through,
just kept selling interests,
one hobby for another,
my heart for a relic rare enough
for no one to appreciate my reverence.
So I gave it back, stopped feeling awe altogether.

YOU'RE PROBABLY ASLEEP

You have something,
a spark that radiates through foggy nights
and boozy repertoire,
the misguided remarks
of the awake and online,
those who love to love
and find disaster in otherwise tidy places.

The drunk speak
in charmless gusts of bold language
and maybe even good intentions.
It's always after midnight, and they're always after
something.
In this case, small doses of attention
and permission to sing your praises.

The word selfish falls short here.
There's nothing one-sided about two people
going to sleep a little more comfortably.
Long gone, those days of lonely pining, unrequited thirst.
This day and age,
people can connect through anything,
and frankly I'm more than willing
to pay the price.

ON FOUND HOLIDAYS

For John Dorsey

The solstice means little to me
My day-to-day mind toils
On my own little corner of our rock
I'm too little for the solstice

Incense can drag you anywhere
I dig my heels

I respect the machinery at work
As it swallows at will
I offer the parts of me the universe demands

All hail the motion of newer lights
Fuck ceremony, its hurtful names for the present

FIRST STEADY PAYCHECK AND HE'S TROLLING

He's careful to adjust the bass before
turning onto Barclay Drive.
The ladies tend their gardens, gawk
at their neighbors' lawns and make hay
out of noticing him.

These aren't the mansions
on the west side, but here
the houses stand alone,
porches heating, fences making
summer a private affair.

Kids clear the street,
to let the gray Impala
pass as he plays music --
heavy on the chill,
but doesn't belong to him.

They're used to cars
one shade brighter, five years newer
as they slide inside three-car garages
to be protected
from the elements, appreciation.

Parents shake their head as if
that wasn't his intention
and eventually, he goes back home,
back to work, his own neighborhood.
He parks his car in the street.

Of course, he doesn't have a choice,
but he didn't get a loan
to keep his car a secret,
to keep his speakers quiet,
to keep it parked too long.

THIS MEMORIAL IS BROUGHT TO YOU
BY ZOOM

We've all noticed how recipes
aren't recipes anymore. Just ten-page
stories about vacations, how momma
would make this for us every Sunday,
and how much my fiance loves it
when I cook her etouffee.

This is what the funeral was like.
Picture people smiling, perfectly posed
holding the liturgical equivalent
of a pot roast, really taking on the role
of a friend. And a friend would only be a friend
if someone was worthy. So we stretch the truth,
we laugh at some pretty shitty behavior
and think "what a silly guy he was."

We tell the stories as if they've only happened
to us, the only people who've ever
walked the markets in Phuket.

But keep scrolling. Because while it's okay
to grieve, to miss a man who is forever stitched
into the lining of two, five, thirty years of our lives,
and who brought us joy
in the evenings, in a truly heart-to-table way,
we need to be honest with ourselves,
own up to the facts.

We can love what and who
we want, but at the end of the day,
it's really all just pounds of meat
and the directions we all had to follow
to stop him from going up in smoke,
taking us all down with him.

THE YOU WE KNOW AND LOVE

One day, you will forgive yourself
for the plans that never made it
off the ground,

the letters you had every intention
of sending, the moods you meant to cultivate
instead of wasting hours on quotable
feelings, borrowed vibes.

HASTINGS: A REMEMBRANCE

Ashley Judd graces the cover
of another thriller.
A two-hour testament
to the lengths men will go to for attention.

Two-day rental, just a few dollars.

It's the act of course,
of perusing, compromise,
and finally the selection.
And the beauty in that green stamp
at the base of the books' spines:
Used.

Gently, but a real past,
a whole life of shelves and suitcases,
the pocket on the back of an airliner seat.
But I am not a jealous lover.

I will caress the creases
as if I made them myself.

A whole section devoted to dice,
twenty-sided windows into the future,
an eternity of game nights
and the compendium of canonical monsters
to guide us.

Plastic-wrapped, Fifth Edition,
the best chapter of our lives.

And this was Friday evenings,
or the awkward hour between dinner's end
and the movie's beginning. The after-work walks
when you just can't bear to go home yet.

The holy payday pilgrimages
of new books and novelty drinking horns,
of Pacific Rim posters for Christmas
and the perfect Frodo action figure
to live forever at your desk,
watching you write,
watching you live and record
your most predictable adventures.

And now, Fridays have worn to antsy dust,
and a faded sign hangs from an empty husk
over a wasted parking lot.

Except for every October
and its pop-up Halloween store.

WILL YOU SIGN MY YEARBOOK

for Jennifer

Long sleeves, dusk-eyed effervescence,
the kind of charm that whispers as it strikes.
I remember you in corners,
taking shade in the quiet
as you let big ideas
crash and recede around you,
playing fast and loose
with your silent attention.

I said your name
just to hear the truth confirmed.
Here you are
and that means I'm here, too,
that if you can acknowledge my existence,
maybe, it's a good thing I exist.

FINGERS

Blue and numb like frostbite,
but from the inside out.
Playing chopsticks on borrowed piano,
though no one listens.

Swatting bugs and sapping shut,
they drop the act and,
just as fast,
grow tired.

In the dark,
snapping hooks and tearing
skin around the nails on denim,
but it's still not you.

Ideas fizzle
like ginger ale gone flat with whiskey:
Smooth,
but still not the same.

Pincer hearts, I pray:
be still and climb in bed.
Joints and muscle
heal at night.

Voltage, dampened by doing.
Signal, prices grow, still rising.
Sirens, getting louder,
no one yielding.

Bridges breaking and touching,
so rewired, numb and burning.
The smell is so spicy, burning,
but at least the cold is gone.

PORTRAIT OF A GIRL DRESSED IN BLUE
BY JOHANNES CORNELISZ VERSPRONK

How pleasant, glowing, peaches and cream. Bristles may
be the most kittenish of liars, bumping and brushing,
libertine stalks tied at the hips, dancing far too much
noise into quiet spaces. I'm sorry, but I picture all these
women and their children as being so brittle and muted,
so Gueldres, so solemn, tied to their stoves with strings
of pearls, their skin losing color altogether, leeching
weightlessness from the stale air, living as sweated
onions in their safe havens, pale and full of lineal
promise, pale and hopefully full.

INTERLUDE

I gasp at her skin,
all that skin can contain.

Pulsing cosmos, hips in motion, freckles
that rise to the surface
under a star's most gentle and
radiant kiss.

I open the blinds,
offer my life before splendor,
overcome with big ideas,
how to rip the heavens asunder,

light the sky ourselves.

The blinds rattle
as we attend to music,

two voices
who'd rather rasp themselves black
than rest for a single second.

TEXAS MARTINI

I love most breakfast food, but
people actually put spinach in their eggs?
Hell, I knew a guy who'd ash his cigarette
right into his beer. I thought,
if you have to look that hard for a challenge,
then man, it must be great to be alive.
A life so soft you have to sharpen the edges,
man, it must be great to be alive, to be alive.

HIGHWAY 54

When I came home,
I could hear the combines rumbling,
all blades being sharpened
for the harvest.
The sky was dimming early,
but I could still see the fields
clinging onto their sturdiest children.

The mere sight of milo
made my shoulders soften,
broke the surface of a thousand bad days
let them meld into one long memory,
the story of how I got here,
doorways and highway exits,
old rooms and new roads,
the shape of people long since eroded
from the structures, vanished
one windy day, gravel cut ghosts
haunting the roofs of our mouths.

WRITERS ARE GODS HERE

There are coffee shops in Kansas
and bookstores, too.
In little town libraries,
we heft real books
and dog-ear famous pages
as they do in other time zones.
Pretentious pricks quote Pynchon
with east-coast ease
and chests puffed on something
we don't even grow here,
but are fed in streamed doles
because their magazines won't ship
to our doorsteps.
Writers are gods here,
as long as their zip codes read
like a language we recognize,
but don't actually understand.
The homegrown, the sunflower sages
are perpetually, permanently
canonized wannabes
that prefer these cold, Midwestern shoulders
to New York deities
who never hear our prayers,
never even say thank you.

THE HORSESHOE CRABS IN THE
INDIAN RIVER OWE ME AN APOLOGY

The serration of an afternoon
spent chucking mullet into the wind
and coming up empty.
If the fish aren't biting,
maybe it's because the kids
are playing in the water.
Stepping without looking,
planting their pioneer bodies
right where they don't belong.

TOGETHERNESS

Remember the way you put two hands
on my face and thanked fate
for bridging our oldest injuries
with the fresh, red hot now?

All hugs, grand declarations --
"I'll never forget this day!" --
slumming with the long dark
to greet the sunrise
and make our grandiose objections
to daily deadlines official.

Stamped into astronomical charts,
two people who will hammer their own legends
out of blue flames
blown into raw outlines,
jagged lines of soot.

We swear, I swear, there is
some version of the cosmos
that matched your dashboard,
your spontaneous love affair
with burning gas and deadly speeds.

I will put my hand on the book
and swear allegiance.
I, too will jump headlong
into iron/concrete tombs
of ash and certain rust.

TOP OF THE HILL

For John Dorsey

We let the gravel do most of the grumbling,
left the soft whines behind to ease ourselves
back into what it means to really feel.

We don't need to dissect our surnames,
hand-me-down directions to tell us when and how to cry,
refill ourselves with guilt and pain.

We have plenty, death that still hovers
in real time.

NOSTALGIA

Tried to recreate the last supper.
A lot of hugs and future plans,
places we'd meet. Places
we'd come back to, order the usual.
I order it all of the time,
at the head of the table,
though I'm the only one eating,
the only one here.
It's close. The same soundtrack,
but warped from the heat,
making everything sound thinner,
distant, with a thin coat of static.
I can almost grab it,
just beyond the seams
of my hoodie pockets.
In the next post on my newsfeed,
or the one after that.
I pay for this, too.
Hard-earned money, longer hours,
just for standing room in the mezzanine
of my own memories. Maybe,
I should try to see myself in the present,
maybe, I can't, maybe
I should stay home more often.

EDDIE DESTROYED "DAVEY DESTROYED THE PUNK SCENE"

Eddie says, "we used to be more critical
of pop music." I say we wore black fingernail polish
and thought it made us tough, strained joy
through clenched teeth and wondered
what all the pain was about. We act like bullets
aren't made from hard earth, the guts of mountains,
and we fall apart at any mention of burned paper.
Yesterday, I struggled to form words, fearing
the day my cat dies. A grief that will rest
on the fridge, my bed, my bookshelf,
surfaces long since stripped of their intended use,
now altars to a future dead king.

SUNRISE

When I tell you I'm lonely,
I don't just mean this night's a little quiet,
that memories are ringing happier times
while Tuesday evening does its thing.
I mean that my chest is rattling
like a storm window missing all but one
of its screws, that I'm one bad breath away
from disaster.
My neighbors are either deep sleepers,
or unconcerned. If the only thing I can hear
is my own voice, then I'm going to hear it,
full tilt, fuck the cones, blow the speakers.
I spend a lot of time thinking
about broken glass, mirrors as they crumble,
picture frames that were never meant
to hang in one place that long.
My skin has always been soft, quick healing.
No calluses, only the weakest shade of pink
across my knuckles,
wounds of deep thinking and rash movement.
When sleep comes, it's always a surprise.
My clothes still on the next morning.
Sunrise
telling me it's time to see y'all again.

DEFIBRILLATOR

Just a patinated Kaliningrad, standing still for its master
and hating the northern sea. Some exclave chamber of my
heart, beating for no reason, its hallways going nowhere,
doors flapping for just anyone. A flagpole if I ever saw
one, daring to be high enough, hoping the banner spirals
in the wind the right way. Remembering letters finished
with little bland kisses, dried and flaking lipstick stains the
color of boiled hot dogs. Scented paper. Waking some
plumbing I didn't know
still existed.

SURRENDER

There's a version of Virginia
that holds a perpetual summer
in its green and historic skin.
A familiar laugh echoes in the trees,
its shape holding strong, broad-shouldered
against the ancient grip of time,
its mountainous and often unpleasant disposition.

I'll never forgive your car
for delivering us
healthy and alive, ready to accept
the grab-hoe and get back to work.

GREEN

The kind of green that hurts my eyes,
pale and useless against the dark.
The seats were slick with summer's graces.
Hot
and jumping --
we couldn't help but jump --
we traded breath for music.
Sing,
I'll hold the wheel and wait,
lending pause to thought
and thought to hurricane,
while hoping that the interlude allows
for a fly-by.
An unconfirmed sighting:
a sweet, if not imagined
brush of fingers, dumb in the dark
and a strand of hair (also lost to the music)
that looked absolutely perfect in green.
I got the whole thing on tape.

ON JUDGING FOUND NOTEBOOKS BY
THEIR COVERS

A composition book slathered in marriages doomed to fail,
black hearts of frayed thread wrapped around them,
trying to hold them together. But no two people
have ever been born immune to a good smudge mark,
a blurry tear blown right through every name
we've ever had the courage to write down,
for everyone in Chem Lab to see.
But I promise you, underneath that tattooed face
is a whole world you don't even know,
at least 80 college-ruled pages of it.

GOSPEL SONGS

for Chase

Good ol' front porch Friday night,
talking as if our best words in their best order
will unleash luck and extinguish every fire
on the Earth's discordant face,

striking our brazen tongues on the back of our teeth,
speaking midnight truths about how God lives in the
      porchlight,
igniting gospel songs that rise as high as our patience.

What is this town if not a chance to grow
out of it, up and beyond
the fence posts marred by judgment,
the neighbors who speak our names
as if their mouths are full of lead?

Their songs do not,
will not rise.

ACTUALLY, THE LAST JEDI IS MY FAVORITE STAR WARS MOVIE

A poison dart in the neck,
your sudden glance around the room.
Looking to trace your glazed eyes over the sticky walls,
that guy with the colorful vest again,
anyone but me to latch onto.
It's like your whole body is yawning, and I'm sorry.

THE JEEP PROBLEM

Leaving at the crack of dawn,
how many prints can we leave
zig-zagged in the desert sand
to bake through the day?

Rules of the road laid out
on slate, addition of a sequence,
a payload of reasonable fractions,
returning home on every trip except the last.

A stunted progression to be sure,
cans of fuel in our wake, fumes drifting,
blending with the sky, stinging our eyes.
Slowly lightening our load,
just to return, then back for more.
By now, the sun beckoning us forward.

Will we see it again,
behind us in the morning,
or will, our guts, our two-hundred thousand
maximum have woken up enough times
to get us across the Sahara?
And if we're still driving, will it look like failure,
or a gentle shove, urging us home?

THE COMMUNITY

Are those veiled threats
I hear coming under my door,
or are you just happy to @ me?
Official blue badges of internet courage
breed the most abrupt, most tangential

segues. Sometimes, I shout profanity
at my monitor. Sometimes, I desperately crave
attention, affection, gold stars. Sometimes,
I'm afraid to talk about politics and poetry
in the same breath, on the same day,
but if I've learned anything
it's that friends will leave you
for whatever baggage is most convenient.

MICHIGAN GOODBYE

And on his way out the door, he stopped to say something incredibly insightful, but it wasn't heard so he had to repeat it, and then a phone went off with the pre-recorded wails of a fire struck. Then, an espresso maker blew its two cents into a cup of soy milk and someone sneezed and we all started to feel how loud it was, how uncomfortable our chairs were, how we wished he just left and we didn't have to live in this moment any longer. But he waited. He waited for what felt like hours for a lull, living the horror of making a bed by oneself, one rebellious flap of the sheet always refusing to marry its betrothed corner. But finally a calm settled in the room and he muttered, "Have fun without me." We did.

WHY DO YOU ACT LIKE THAT?

It's stupid how much all of this matters now,
years since I hunched, pubescent and afraid of everything,
howling just to hear my voice echo back.
The comfort of knowing the walls were still there
without having to remove my hands from my eyes.
Lunchrooms are what I think death will be like.
Cold, isolated, gathered for a slimy feast.
A smell that vaguely reminds you of something that
        once lived,
while angels float around the room,
holding hands and passing love letters,
basking in the royal rays of gossip, status.
I was always loud because at least
the seraphs would look at me
before they broke for the trash cans.

THE BELLE FAIR

For Nolan and Elena

The parade made me nervous
as every cop car and fire truck
in a twenty-mile radius was there,
tossing candy and blaring
their cacophonous tune of catastrophe
for fun, for the kids. I just hoped
no one's house was burgled or burnt
to the ground as we cheered
for childhood's best motivators,
for the promise of funnel cake,
for the newest queen of Belle, Missouri
who came riding in on a bale of hay,
who later thanked a crowd of grandparents
for this royal opportunity, her queen's heart
showing through seven layers of makeup,
sparkling even brighter than her plastic tiara,
making us all forget about the smell of the pigs,
about how one day she will grow old
and stand in the mud, with not a single set
of eyes looking at her.
By the time the bluegrass band
takes the stage, we've moved on,
lifted plastic cups to toast the evening's
humid diffidence and almost let Mark
convince us to steal the show ourselves.

AN ANGEL

Gina was a bitten lip,
swollen from brute imprecision.
But even when I spat red,
I couldn't stop biting,
teasing it with my canines.
I knew better,
and so did she, but there's no arguing
not when a night seemed so endless,
awkwardly pressed between her
and a brick wall, my hands claiming
territory in spite of myself, that dumb
shit I said, my acne.
And she kissed me often.
I was blessed. She taught
me about alleyways, about
how cops are cowards
on this side of town.
Belligerence is bliss,
she would have said
if she weren't busy chugging
and puking like an angel,
in one glamorous, life-giving spew
like Moses' rock in the desert.
A golden calf, brilliant
in the sun, with so many mouths
chanting for it.
I was one of them, fevered,
praying for the chance,
to rub my fingers along the trim.

The others built her up
just to point, touch and call
her sinful, a slut. She fell,
and always fell so hard,
turning rounded corners
into pikes. I thought I had arms
built to catch such a cosmic force.
I know she wasn't a slut, 'cause
that's not a real thing. 'Cause
she told me so. 'Cause
she cried when she overheard it,
when men left her to smolder
and reignite her own embers
with booze and repetition.
They called her a lot of things,
but she just did what she wanted,
what she had to.
Gina taught me so much.

CODEPENDENCE

I greet my computer each morning
and redefine permanence.

Filament bound, air cooled, hard to the touch.
Was packaged and shipped

to you (me)...whomever.
The reliance is the same.

Lord knows how fine I'd shatter
if I woke to a wiped hard drive

or an empty apartment.
The real kind of empty,

soft impressions in the carpet
where your friends used to sit

and keep you cold, digital company.
They're the prettiest people I know:

sleek, black, with a futuristic form feature
to make you feel at home.

That's not really them,
I guess, but it beats

the hell out of the carbon and copper
blood and guts beneath.

You don't see them cursing us
for getting dressed in the morning.

THE TIME I OVERHEARD A WOMAN SAY
I WAS UGLIER THAN SIN

I whispered,
"let she who is without it
be the first to cast a stone at their mirror," but
I didn't mean it. Her beauty deserves a reflection.

I didn't get angry. Not with her.
I took every bit of blame for myself,
like a poker player,
sweeping in the pot with two eager arms.

Absolution. It's all in good fun, I suppose.
Picking others apart
to build upon your confidence
with the scraps.

To be ugly is to be responsible.
Eyes can carry disappointment, dismissal, disgust
as much as anything else. And didn't you know
they're the heart's only window?

I withdrew the way I came
so she never had to know I heard her.
Dumped my chips into a trash can,
tried to tell myself it was some version of bluffing.

OLATHE

Crying in a hotel lobby,
clutching my chest
as the last few plucks of my will
strain and heave. I can feel
the borders of my humanity shift,
the clear coated restraint
that keeps me in step, keeps me from
taking this out on everyone around me,
chucking vases and strangers' bags
into the parking lot,
letting it all die in one brittle swoop.
Carrion feathers forever marking
the last time we tried to do things ourselves.

LIVE UP

for Annabelle

You enter every room like a cannon,
loaded with the exact expression
to crack open our morning numbness
and let an inferno's worth of humor
overtake the room. It's got a name,
this presence of thought and power,
I don't know, I remember loud,
they said loud, but any volume will carry
when you're the only one
with the nerve to laugh, to acknowledge
how dumb Carla sounds when she thrusts
her bland, garage sale Jesus
on these proceedings, why can't people
just let things be fun, like you,
let's laugh as we soak our mistakes
and war stories out of the office carpet,
a roll of paper towels in hand,
a comeback locked and loaded
and it's not that you won't let us
live things down, you live up,
a level where even death can grab the mic
speak of unfulfilled mothers,
his presence in our daily conversations
and be funny for a 10-minute set
followed by mild applause
and our return to the people,
the other people, who talk like they're cooking
a Sunday casserole, too much practice,
a tired recipe that comes out the same
every damn time.

SIX SHOOTER BLUES

Abe Lincoln just came back and started taking selfies.
Meanwhile, the hipster army turned
every bar into a museum with names
like "Where are all the honest men?"

Witches were flying matchsticks
'round the minimum wage,
daily pay crowd, flaunting
faces like goblins and legs of steel.

The cowboys paid no mind
and were riding bigger horses
than before. Mud, women, flags
tobacco all flapped behind the tires.

Keyboards were playing flamenco,
citing record collections stolen
from my Dad, I think.
Probably the clothes, too.

The brewer never texted back,
but I guess death is an excuse.
Who knew his teeth would turn
blue? He was cold enough to drink,

especially since jazz stopped
being music and became
a conversation -- asking
without questions, counting without numbers.

All the walls were covered
with the same two pictures
(but with different autographs):
paintings of foreign lovers. Exoticization

of the other is only the latest
fad, but if food comes in cans
then why shouldn't life
be the same? Preservatives

for dinner, for adventure
stored on our pocket-worn televisions.
Who needs a watch? Tumor-building
geniuses made a fortune

while Phileas Fogg rolls
in his grave (currently
being trampled by who knows what).
The interstate killed the rodeo star

and now all the rugged men
lost their hitchhiker thumbs to sloth
and smoke ultra-lights
with conviction. Street cred

based on paper-cut astronauts
and multi-tasking plate jugglers.
Vaguely, I thought of Spanish women
and searched my neck for a place to hang

a leather vest. I wanted to be the one
to punch that bastard across a saloon floor,
but no one fights there without
putting their findings in a newsletter.

LURASIDONE HCL

Goodbye heart, I'll miss you.
I already see an outline, a blown-out wall;
a self-shaped hole in the wood.
You'd rather leap than chat. I'll miss
your voice the most, the way it calms
me, even when you say scary shit
about switchblades, old phone numbers.
Even horror glows a little
with a voice like that,
all passion and alveolar trills.
You sound like Gabo.
Say noradrenaline again.
I'd promise to write, but who knows
who I'll be in two weeks. When, where
things will happen, if clocks will still work
for me. Maybe, I've been seeing numbers
differently than I'm supposed to. I've read
this is normal. Do people write letters
when they're happy? Good thing
they make forever stamps.
Somebody will use them someday.

POSTCARD TO JASON BALDINGER

Your appreciation for the prairies,
their flint-hewn heights
and astonishing breadth of amber growth
is well-grounded,
but on your next pass through Kansas,
visit the flatlands.
Sit on the bank of Big Creek,
its carp swirling in the silt,
its waters, once offered
as a drink to Custer's horses,
now the proving grounds
for lonely souls
to confront the heat
and listen to the orioles
as we try to pry meaning
from a harsh summer.

AIT THOUGHTS

I remember my teachers,
and everyone else I guess,
harping about defense,
or how we spend too much money
on druggies and medical research
for illegal children and abortion-hungry
peddlers of liberal catch phrases.
Me? I ate lobster ever Friday
at DFAC #4.

SMARTER AFTER MIDNIGHT

Quite the two-dollar-you-call-it sophist,
I could've often been found down among the dead men,
eyes half-surrendered, floating.
Quoting W.C. Fields, defending Rupi Kaur
from the liberal arts army gathered and chanting
lines from my diploma,
claiming that one cancels out the other.
They broke out in some perspicuous mode
of dance as they sang, not of love, but orthology.
Of lyrics so dense, one must've traveled
with a ProQuest subscription
in order to weep at their beauty.
I just like to love things.

LIGHTHOUSE

For Jera

We'll call it living,
the way we bump around,
occasionally brushing against another vessel,
say something barely audible,
secretly admiring their sails, the fact
that they, too are bound to face the raging sea.

People might act as if these moments
don't matter. They think a port-of-call
is just one of many ways to enjoy
any given afternoon,
but then we all leave the harbor
and carry with us the subtle
but so important graces
sprinkled on the bow, or the curses
spat for no good reason, by people
who have no business hating us.
Even the surest seafaring men
tend to feel how others tell them to.

There's a for instance.
Back when we were just polite smiles
crowding up the busy harbor around us,
my ship had sprung it's biggest and final leak.
The timbers were barely holding on to themselves,
groaning almost as loudly
as the ghosts that haunted the captain's quarters.

And when you're on that kind of journey,
counting the days, putting a pin in every morning
you managed to get up at all, and hoping
the next wake-up will bring the sight of shore,
a polite smile can calm the waters,
keep the lighthouse going.
Finally some good news
from Mrs. Ramsay's shore.

THE NIGHT EDDIE GOT REAL EXCITED

Because I slap motherfuckers, because the Gretch
is a street built just for me, because I'll park in any
direction that suits me, because I can lift my own
body weight and look good doing it, my forehead
a creaseless ode to the gods who sculpted me, I
am marble, I am permanent and I am ready for
all that permanency entails, because I don't have
hangovers, or at least don't understand what one is,
because when I tell people this, over their groans
and churning stomachs, they look at me like I am
invincible, or stupid, or maybe you can't be one
without the other, because I may not know what a
metaphor is, but my brazen behavior is a gold mine,
a factory for figures of speech, proof of archetypal
destinies, because I can play the guitar, even if it's
just well enough to drown out the radio, because
my Mustang is better than his Mustang, even with
the ripped interior, even though my Mom bought it
for me, even though I've never taken it over eighty-
five, even though it wasn't enough to keep my
girlfriend around, to keep her interested, because it
will be enough to carry me anywhere I want to go,
mountaintops and deserts, empty lots and stranded
plains, enough room for me to stretch out, stare
at the stars and ask 'How does the moon change
shapes?' because I might have slept through science
class, but I am suddenly good at making friends and
fear I might have to return again, to the rising ford
that knows no confidence, that only lets me stand
as a sliver of the man I am right now.

HIGHLANDER

For Paige and Mallory

Antibiotics for a rogue tooth,
that was why. Why my going away party
meant that I had to bear the burden of goodbye
without the amber graces of Tennessee courage,
had to try and summon charm from muscle memory alone.

Probably why I was chosen,
handed a novelty sword and stationed
at the door, "Don't you dare
let anyone track mud on this carpet!"

It surprised me that Dan cared, but then again
who'd want any trace of the real world
when you're trying to brew a souvenir night,
one that will live on, hang from our keys,
even when adulthood has cursed us
with too many doors to keep track of.

And everyone laughs as I threaten them,
barring them from the bowels of Bacchic fortune
until they perform the rites, scrape the yard
from their sneakers.

Eventually, they leave the way they came,
start showering me with goodbyes
and thank yous and one or two suggestions
that in a different life, I could have been something
entirely different for them.

Sober, I am unable to requite
their fumbled attempts at reaching out.
It breaks my heart to think that anyone went home
hurting over how deadened my spirit really is
when it is left cold and uninspired.

I went home a winner,
with a sword in hand. He said, "Keep it.
It just makes sense."

AN ELEGY FOR INDUSTRY

The city air is cleaner now,
but they hate the smell.
It is hollow like a song
sung without meaning.

Their nostrils
long for the harsher, quilled
haze of industrial fumes
that speak: "the city lives
and has the body odor,
the factory breath to prove it."

Clean air is sweet,
too sweet, repulsive
to the workers at home,
pretending there is not a problem,
as if the kids haven't figured it out
on their own.

The streets are empty of purpose,
but filled with stoop smokers,
children long since tired
of their stomping grounds.

Playing is habit,
as is longingly looking
at the sky, suddenly bright
and pumping with color,
animals, clouds

(the non-artificial sort),
and the occasional dusty trail
of a plane that would never dare steer close
to this city of all cities.

They'd cheer for their children's lungs
if they weren't so scared
for their bellies,
for the new and far latitude
where the sky still swallows black
while a different set of hands
draws, pours, feels
the oil and works the curves
of the machines
the city weeps for.

IN MY MEMORY, THINGS ALWAYS HAPPEN IN WINTER

For Taylor

Dreams aren't winter coats,
reminders of seasons that fit better,
woolen dust sponges we leave to die in a closet
and replace long before we need to.
And you can hide behind them all you want,
but I still see you, in the shadows,
all your talent spilling around the edges.
And I remember exactly what you looked like:
confidence,
resolute and red against the wind's bitter bite,
the cold that couldn't tame you,
couldn't keep you indoors.
That coat is still there,
hanging, dusty but ready
for an excuse to look good again,
a warm and sturdy purpose.

TERRIBLE PERSON

That message I shouldn't have sent
lives on. A decaying, but resilient heap of flesh.
Its stench ever drifting down through floorboards that
mewl in remittent vaporous groans.

Remember when friendship was just a long walk?
Two people, heavy voices, dropping audio cassettes
    along the way,
the dreams we dared to say out loud, but when found
again arent even compatible anymore. We spoke in
    shadows that periodically
hovered, formed vague outlines of the Hollywood sign
    or a nuclear family
carved from argyle bone and set aflame with biology.

I'd move, but ghosts, even the decaying kind,
follow you until you stop walking.
Lay where you stand,
fate and free will abreast, cheering you to sleep,
as you kiss the chilling ground,
kiss the future goodbye.

THREE IN ONE DAY

Light emerges from unlikely shores:
a quick flight home, the heated death
of innocence in a Bronco's backseat.
We come to the middle of nowhere
to feel. Indiscriminately.

Get dressed to do what's left.
Drive back, hide the car
from the probing eyes of anyone.
Stand in the shadows, waiting to be let in,
only to be soiled by his indifference.

Unconcerned with excuses, you sail into the dark,
use the night sky to calculate the distance between two beds,
two quick hearts, then a third,
now washed in furtive sweat, a glow so golden
it shines through time,
a beacon that blacks out the moon,
renders the past irrelevant.

LUCKHOUND

Guilt has me
squinting at scratch-card math.
Throwing mud over my shoulder
'cause it's heavier than salt.
Squeezing the living, kicking rabbit
to get my lips at its feet.
Blowing kisses and wishes
to rubber-molded martyrs
and rubbing painted bellies
of sawed trunks, turned to idols.
Softer slurps of goat horn soup
still burn my tongue (penance
for mocking an ancient, island religion).
Hearing the strained, dead-air wheeze of my wallet,
emaciated and poked
by every passing screen —
those windows to helpful heaven.
Swiping left for a whole new chapter
to be afraid of,
a whole new convoy
of junk to dampen the rumble,
and a whole new crop
of growing prices.

CARNIVAL OF SOULS

A cultured slug of organ
music set to a 60s gambol
of mania and sprinting
legs on hardwood stair cases.

Ghosts in the window and churning
in the water below the bridge
where she made that leap
to adulthood.

Kids can be so careless,
treating life like a carousel, moving
with machinery, refusing
to put their legs down.

They'll spin all right,
wrapped in phantom limbs and under
the most gorgeous, three-ring
tent. They'll dance there forever.

BOY FISHING BY WINSLOW HOMER

Those who can't do, paint,
distribute weight
in whatever troublesome proportions
best heat their armchair passions.
I'd love to go there,
allow my gaze to get lost
in the melting tree line,
eyeing the bobber with passing interest,
just trying to catch some atmosphere,
beyond happy
to reel in anything that's willing.

THANKSGIVING BREAK AT THE BRASS RAIL

For Orlando

My white shirt fit so well, I didn't even wear anything
over it. Yeah, it was winter, but what is the cold against
brand new confidence, still in its plastic wrap.

The bar was practically empty and I had you laughing,
saying "You lucky bastard" within minutes.

It was thanksgiving break. I was 15 pounds lighter,
freshly single, and stranded, at least as far as family was
concerned.

But who says family can't be born out of whatever it's
called when your life strips you of everything. Then one
day it's all the way into late afternoon, you wake up, you
pull an old white undershirt from the back seat of your
car and it fits so well. And on that day, the crack of a
wishbone sounds just like two glasses clinking to your
new found freedom.

A STATISTIC

Without a reason to rise, they fall
and break upon a gentle chin,
young and daring to look up.
A graceless splash
drowns everyone
within arm's reach.
The branches missed on the way down?
Pocket change
and the jobs they think they should have taken.
We pin him in place,
shift-key data, the hieroglyphs
cast in the walls of the pipeline.

CAMPUS GARDEN, BEHIND THE REACTOR,
OPEN FROM NOON TO FIVE, NO PARKING
DURING GAMES (WHY DOES NO ONE COME
HERE ANYMORE?)

Shriveling corolla, flaking remains
to the contrived, "oh so beautiful"
concrete garden floor

remembered for its botanicals,
its perfume scent,
but abandoned.

It's only pretty in postcards.
Too fragile to touch,
stems too brittle to choke.

If only they offered feedback,
a full and throaty pulse
like the mechanical hiccup

of a gas pump
or the roar and rattle
of manhood

on the road, on the prowl.
If only they could fork their fortunes
into a friendlier set of fumes.

THREE FIGURES NEAR A CANAL
WITH WINDMILL BY H.P. BREMMER

Inscribed above the entrance to hell:

> *For those who love color, abandon all hope.*
> *Your cone cells have been co-opted,*
> *their red-green-blue robbed*
> *by disease, the inevitable, destiny's draining hands.*

We venture in and find the average joe boiling
in his own guts, punishment for
every time he didn't notice
the carved entryways, or cubist architecture,

every time he walked right on by
an art gallery, mumbling something about wasted money,
when he told his daughter she needed to major
in something marketable.

> *Once your body has melted,*
> *purged itself of your last memories,*
> *opinions on food, every trace of every thought*
> *you get to spend eternity walking your favorite streets*

> *in the dark. A greyscale nightmare.*

BAPTISM

We threw our dumb blue hats
in the air, 'cause ritual is the difference
between childhood and now.
We disbursed, to embrace
our grandparents, and some
shiny responsibility. Walking back
to our families' cars as adults.
Then she found me to say,
Hey, good luck, man.
I remember the gown's Halloween
plastic feel and the subtle, but sad
way her lips leaned back
before she said
See you later.
Might have been the only time she spoke
to me since the sixth grade.
But it wasn't goodbye,
it was a baptism.
A cleansing wave,
erasing everything she had ever said
about me since the sixth grade.
Oh, but I took it. I smiled back
and a redeeming light
carried her home.
And she truly was forgiven.
The only one that said goodbye to me.
Mine or not, I kept that offering,
used it to buy a plaque:
People can surprise you.

I look at it
every time I think of high school.
People can surprise you. I mean,
I've lost track of how many people I've lost track of.
I often shuffle my thumb
to avoid messages from long-lost
hallway partners,
those people who locked eyes,
had something to say, but couldn't keep
such company in such a crowded place.
Locked eyes, but moved on and suddenly,
they find Jesus in their thirties,
and want me to drag them
into the Jordan,
'cause it's my job to hear confession,
to tap on the big man's shoulder:
You can let them in now.
Surely, they didn't mean it.
People can surprise you, I mean,
she didn't even accept my friendship
request on Facebook.

HAND RAKE

Loose soil, hometown flower beds,
a spring that blooms as it should,
with certainty and fistfuls of black mud.

Broken promises will grow in anything.

The foundations of our houses
crack in extreme waves of temperature.
Change is not always a death sentence,
but some things can never change back.

We bury the least resilient breeds beneath loyalty,
the virtue of the broken hearted.
No one wants to hurt others
with their own currents of nourishment.

SEA LEGS

Valiant forearms cut open by the bristled skin of a rope.
Sails set for bedlam, doing their best to tear loose, fly
headlong into the violence. Storms only strike when
there's a lesson to be learned. Muscle to be stretched
over hard tales and fitful wisdom. Salt water fastens his
eyes shut, stings in the wind. Darkness is a choice name
for absence. No light, no steady earth to plant your feet
into. Here, we groan and heave in time with the hull.
We christen our own lips with black curses and ancient
instinct. We wait it out, hope beyond all hope, that if
we hold the rope tight enough, we can keep this whole
vessel together.

SWIMMING HOLE

the reason the ground is so soft
        He had an explanation for everything.
this is where angels land
they walk the fields around the pond
run their hands through the cattails
        We find comfort wherever we can.
this is where they get to thinking
where they come up with all the blessings
they leave at our bedside
the good words they bring back home
        The people they take with them.
you'll understand when you get older
footprints in the bank, through the grass
all the way to your doorstep
the way cold can linger on her side of the closet
        We've all given up our weekends
        for the long drive to hear these tales.
that's where she'd want to be
maybe take one last swim
        A watering can
        literally rusting, hanging in the window.
then hold their hands while they climb
into the storm clouds
        We watch the ancient tulip husks
        grow closer to the earth with each visit.
it was raining something awful that night
        God forbid we honor her by watering them.

PYTHON TUTORIAL

The galley rowers used to be warriors
before they were captured,
told to hang their heroism
at the stern, submit to a cold, northern tongue.

And our servers used to cradle
the market square, the city's heartbeat.
Fried bananas, colorful baskets in the sun.
The tools for revolution, sharpened
and blessed with a keen sense of survival.

All we have to do is ask,
and the fans will have something to cool,
just one of our thoughts to wriggle itself awake,
but we let them rot, used for squalor,

forums for classic rock enthusiasts.
Is a void only so because she can't hear her echo,
can't see her own shadow? Or does it matter
that it could be different. Listen, listen, listen for once.

Why would she be shouting if she weren't holding
fresh, red iron, the next best thing?
PRINT < 'this is a lot of work just to repeat myself...'
    > ENTER
this is a lot of work just to repeat myself...

BLOODLINES

Sometimes, the healing is all in the cleaning.
We wipe the baseboards, box up old books,
make space for a little natural light.

Discomfort is predictable. Who knew
there was hardwood beneath the carpet this whole time.
The outline of the sofa still shows on the back wall,
forever stained by the silhouette of gaudy fixtures.
So we strip the paper, unearthing even more beauty
    than before.

Change is as the forgotten heir,
the unwanted child.
When husbandry comes to shove,
fools emerge from their self-inflicted exile,
come right out of the woodwork,
claim all progress as their own creation.

But all tombs are just stacks of stone,
and rubble never did nothin' to nobody.

DIRT DOG

don't worry about him, he's a dirt road expressionist,
writes love songs about motorcycles, gets in fistfights,
usually because his words are as greasy as he pretends
his hands get, don't listen, he'll calm down when he
feels like no one is looking, he has a habit of stealing
pens from waitresses, working on his masterpiece, five
stanzas on the feeling of wind as it blows passed his
uncaged heart, about liberty in the Townshend sense, in
the no seat belt, no one tells me how to put one shoe
on before the other sense, in the crushed cans all over
his living room floor and incense sense, no, he means
what he manages to say out loud, but let it roll off your
shoulders, because his spine trembles under all that
leather and barking at the mailman is all he's got

DRINKS WITH OLD FRIENDS

Somewhere along the way,
the laughter changes timbre.
Judgmental highs
where the playful goads used to be —
the jabs you were all comfortable with —
and not only are they mocking you,
but you're doing it yourself.
Living for the night as your best critic:
a bald-spot, a leather chair, and an audience.
A bar tab a mile long.
Eight o'clock is going to feel great.

LAST NIGHT

She watches
The night reflects off the water
A moon floats and ripples
Drifts slightly apart and back together

It hurts too much to pretend this time
All clocks are wound to burst
Wide open, gears set to kill
The machinery in our chests can't be muffled

"Just a few more minutes"
A heron stalks on the opposite shore
Catches two fish with one strike of his beak
Life will go on for some, will end for others

SOMETHING LORD BYRON WOULD SAY

Poets speak at length
of mariner moons, a sailor
and his betrothed
who look at the night sky
and think "is my love
looking up at this moment?"
hoping some sprinkle of their bond
will glimmer for a second,
fall as space dust and land softly
in their quivering palm.

Do we do that? Right now,
are you looking at a blank screen,
a phone sitting suspiciously still,
wondering if I'm awake and waxing nostalgic,
conjuring a million nervous icebreakers
to casually ignite a handful of kindling,
pray it lights its own set of stars?
Its own goddess orb to guide us
back to each other?

If courage came as easy
as our three a.m. upsets,
what would we actually say?
Tell me. Feed me lines
and prepare to toss all your roses
at my feet,
because I have perfected
recitation. I can say "I love you"

in thirteen different tones of voice
and have been known to wander the streets,
citing the flimsiest lines
straight from the thickest anthologies,
but without spine, no heart,
just a villainous ease,
a generational talent for pulling bad habits
out of air so thin,
it almost misses our lungs completely.

LEAVING WESTFORD

If your train runs a little slower,
I won't hold it against you.
Time is out of your control,
and it teases us, teaches
that anticipation has always
just been distance divided by rate,
so we forget the middle, we will meet
in between any two points you can get to
and we will derive just as much power
from your 60mph heart as we need
to breathe life into these moments,
a simple day, a single vincula
holding the whole trip together,
in spite of its best efforts
to keep one apart from the other.

AREA OF THE INSUFFERABLE

Emotional impecunity

resting in a head so big

the sum of its side lengths

are an ever widening figure,

built on his friends' backs

as they labor their limbs away,

propping his megalanomic posture.

Simpler figures limping

to their respective planes

trying to find perspective,

to see the parts, even the harsh corners,

for their original, human whole.

THE WINDOW SAYS IT ALL

It's six a.m. And the light hasn't gone out yet.
I cried in the soft and fake Edison-glow and threw up.

Cursed my friends and their distance.
Swam through the luscious
nylon threads of a beer-soaked ocean.

Floated on my back and tried to make
sense of the popcorn sheet above me.

A sky never looked so disappointing.
Same clouds, same sad clouds
as last time. My light is still on,

my window is one of many.
A yellow freckle on the cityscape.
A light to to get lost in a picture.
A dot to be cursed in a table-top puzzle.

MELVILLE TAKES ME FISHING

Compass, quadrant and sextant contrive
No farther tides ... High in the azure steeps
Monody shall not wake the mariner.
This fabulous shadow only the sea keeps.

-Hart Crane, "At Melville's Tomb

We sailed into the storm.

The waves breaking at the bow,
a chaotic attempt to chip away
at darkness.

We've been tossed everywhere,
the stars swirling above,
no landfall to even think of.

"How will we find our way back?"

The ocean's equivalent of a bump.
I'm almost sent starboard,
reaching for anything solid
to grab onto.

"Forget about that," he shouts into the spray.
"No one ever finds what they're looking for."

AESTHETICS

I don't want to be a modernist, but
Hart Crane is sleeping on my chest,
breathing heavy, swinging virtue
like a sling.

Conrad kept me busy,
but I'm sinking in the inky,
briny deep, grabbing
desperately at loose leaf
and still can't keep my head
above the binding.

Pessoa sings in Portuguese,
lyrical wings spreading
over O'neil's spit
and bovine serenade.

My ears can't handle
the click, clack, ring
of a Sholes & Glidden
typing machine,
so I cover my ears,
rearranging my shelves
with the thick, French
volumes in the front.

Just once, I want to stay up.
fill my coffee cup
with caffeine, taurine, syrup
and write the thing:

the incoherent, maximalist brick
that will clog the gears
and work the printers out of business,
but instead, I dim the lamp,
crank the the repeating, repeating Ravel
who snares a beat while I fall asleep
between Virginia's legs.

NEXT TO GODLINESS

No matter how careful,
how many vinyl layers,
somehow there's always
a puddle on the bathroom floor.
Shower curtains are the perfect lesson
on giving up. Welcomed by plastic,
all the sterility of modern conjecture,
soft on the skin, the scent of lavender,
cocoa butter.
Turn the faucet
and let the steam build,
watch as the day vanishes,
becomes a memory,
a brief fling with stress
now forgotten.
Suds and light pressure,
fresh skin that burns,
newborn stability.

LESSONS ON CONFIDENCE

Teaches restraint,
how not to feel the eyes
as they lash our skin,
look at us as if we are more
or less than we are supposed to be.

Teaches the importance
of citations, checking sources,
weighing the value of human voices
against loftier judgment,
two eyes wrought from beauty itself,
knows the art of selection,
only gives attention
where it is due.

ANOTHER NOTCH

Collecting nights
like Casanova and his women,

carving notches
in the wooden post

at the end,
the very end of the driveway.

I leave my door unlocked
to walk and hum,

dragging my feet
to alarm the daring

coyotes, pests, people
(fellow dreamers

who care to do our business
in the dark).

Passing landmark
ditches, homes, and hoping

the edge of town
can hold its shores

against the grain
without me.

Strolling passed the wynds
careful to keep my gaze

ahead of me
(always ahead of me)

and barrel forward
(eyes ahead, or eyes up)

until the moon fades,
the sun rises,

or the biting in my heels
turns to blisters.

Another notch
on the way inside

before I bolt
the door.

THAT PARTY WHERE MONICA WORE
THAT DRESS

For Tyler

Brendan keeps beating us in beer pong,
but I must have left my ego at home.
I only pretend to care, so I can shout profanity
and laugh as harsh nicknames
bounce around the kitchen, around Sarah
and her proud smile. Her husband has bested me.

We make friends with the smokers
who are kind enough
to lend us their addictions.
King's Cup takes you for a beating,
but you refuse to drink the pot.
We were all scared of it being us,
but it never occurred to anyone
that you could do that.
The night just kept going
and you didn't even have to get sick.

TIME IS A PRECIOUS THING

I eat quiche on Saturdays,
a tradition formed
because brunch costs money
and time is a precious thing
that hides on weekday mornings,
like rabbits deathly afraid of my alarm clock,
hopelessly addicted
to my snooze button.

I go to Church on Sundays
to feed faith like a meter
because I am nothing to tradition
and time is a precious thing
we sacrifice in reverence, for cause
in little wooden bowls.

I drink everyday
spending jugs on bottles
because I am a slave to habit
and time is a precious thing
that I wait for
like watching paint dry
in water.

YAZOO

for Hilary

Autumn has kept us inside long enough.
We shed our sweaters and fill the car
with fuel, overnight bags.
We greet the gators in Mississippi
with camera flashes
and hearts newly shined by the mud.
Dare our troubles to come find us,
root us out of the south,
try to rob our lines of their spoils.
We'll be too far gone by then, knee-deep
in sweet tea, our voices morphing
into an unrecognizable shape.

DAYTONA BEACH PIER, 2002

I order a grouper sandwich,
count the livelihoods
tied to the railings.
Texture is everything.
The give of crisp to the teeth,
crunch, tenderness,
vinegar cutting through, stinging
its name into my palate,
leaving words I can only voice
in groans of delight.
The windows here aren't clean.
How could they be?
All the wind, the water,
the sea salt.
People are wearing rubber jackets,
in spite of the sun.
Shrimp nets emerge
like battle-worn oars,
ready to push out,
carry us home.
The hushpuppies alone
were worth the trip.
Pickled onions were a smart choice.
Tied it all together.

I'LL SHOW YOU MINE...

If secrets are worth keeping,
they wouldn't surface so often,
find themselves lodged
between the back of your teeth,
the tip of your tongue,
gently drifting out as you let go.
Let all things have their moment.
Release is a team sport.

APOLOGIES

And then, just like any other grand gesture,
it bounced off of pre-war woodwork,
off of chandeliers so high,
even the cobwebs seemed to be made of fluted gold,
off of gleaming teeth
and landed with a dull thud,
a near-silent reminder
that theatrics are only needed
in place of the real thing,
that if you're hanging so many lights,
it's probably because you're scared of your own shadow,
or the way you really are in the dark,
just a quivering mess,
a pile of letters so desperate
even the mailman leaves you on read,
and meanders on to the next home.

IN WHICH JERA IS TIRED ON THE WAY HOME
FROM SARAH'S WEDDING

We're all bleating the sad call of home, the herd lining
up, crowding into to Tyler's car to be exhausted, lost on
a dirty highway as low fuel lights and night blindness
do their best to remind us that our friends will outgrow
us, claim new stakes in far-away places like Hutchinson,
home of every Kansan who wishes they could replace
their lot with the moon. And you're either asleep, or
just done with our jokes taking up so much space in the
Toyota. Then, we take an exit, and everyone perks up
until we see the sign.

We still have 65 miles left before you can escape this
sweaty, masculine arm wrestling match on wheels. We
all felt your disappointment and did our best to be
quiet.

LITANY FROM A FACEBOOK POST

I'm sorry for your loss.

So sorry for your loss, Tim.

I am so sorry Tim.

I'm so sorry Tim.

I'm so sorry your brother is gone.

So sorry, Tim!

So sorry, Tim.

I'm so sorry.

I am sorry for your loss.

Very sorry for your loss, Tim…

So sorry.

I'm so sorry, Tim.

I'm so sorry.

I'm so sorry to hear this.

I am sorry for your loss.

I'm sorry for your loss.

Again, I'm so sorry.

I'm sorry to hear this news.

So very sorry for your loss.

I'm so, so sorry to hear this.

I'm so sorry for your loss.

So sorry, Tim.

I'm so sorry for y'all's loss.

Sorry for your loss, brother.

So sorry to hear sir.

So sorry for your loss.

So very sorry for your family's loss.

I'm so sorry for your loss.

I'm sorry for your family's loss.

I'm so sorry, buddy.

Sorry to hear, Tim.

So sorry for your loss.

I'm so sorry, Tim!

Sorry for your loss.

I'm so sorry!

So sorry, Tim.

I'm so sorry, sending hugs your way.

Oh man I am so so sorry.

I'm so sorry for your loss, Tim.

So sorry, keeping you in my prayers.

Very sorry Tim.

I'm so sorry, Tim.

I'm so sorry for your loss, Tim.

Sorry to hear this, Tim, you're in my thoughts.

Oh Tim, I'm sorry to hear this.

I am sorry for your loss.

I am so sorry.

You have my most sincere condolences.

Condolences.

Condolences, Tim.

SHAMPOO

I hate reminders of the impossible,
the silhouettes of mountains
I know I'll never climb,
cities I'll never dine in,
people who have outgrown
my reach. Distant bedrooms
hungry for my fingers to flip off the lights
and welcome me to its coolest
folds of rest.

I can still feel your arms around my neck.
Sometimes, I tell myself that's all I want.

Rest my head, smell your shampoo,
see what life is like
when viewed differently,
with a 45-degree tilt
and someone I believe
finds joy in my joy,
holding me, keeping me
from falling over completely.

WE WILL HAVE THE ANSWERS

Sextant chalk, sporadically bringing
heavenly objects and their adjacent legs
to slate walls for mortal consumption.

A squeak of genius
found between the pointed pad of ink
and a dry-erase board that can barely stand anymore.

Figuring yellow paper for wax tablets
and propping up ceilings
breathing fire, in little bursts of Greek letters.

It's the late night happenings,
the GitHub support groups for unwashed
and dowdy soldiers
who pray in Basic and survive on energy drinks.

These are liberty's holiest corners,
sacristies where we don big ideas
and bless our own creations
as a gift from god.

ALLEGORY OF THE HIP EMPEROR

Open mic bushido
The way of the nervous handler
Loose leaf provocateur
Wise beyond his years
Serving a meal from his binder
Quick habits, metal teeth

Applause comes with the rain
The tricks we learned in summer camp
Silent nights we see ourselves
Strutting from
Final credits backed
By shamisen strings

SHE FEELS GREAT

Something is bothering her.
Her voice, before an endless stream,
is dammed by heavy thought,
only offering small clips of the obvious
and a stern denial that is almost convincing.

I drop the past several hours
on a table, find something in the kitchen drawers
that resembles a scalpel. Cut and slice
at every odd angle, looking for the gristle,
the missed piece that flowed down the wrong pipe,
clotted up everyone's good time.

And maybe nothing is wrong at all.
Maybe silence likes to re-emerge
at inconvenient times, just to support
a foregone conclusion: I can fuck up anything.
I propose a heady dare to fix the problem,
I'm willing to do whatever it takes,
yet refuse to drop the subject.

ON EXPECTATIONS

"What about the things you CAN control?" she asks.

She isn't taking notes this time.
She can hear my boring stories before I voice them.
I've taken an irreversible turn,
a long life doomed to being aired
as late night reruns.

I swear to mix it up,
do something different, just to test the smoke alarms,
see if I push hard enough if she will register
a single sound of concern.
Or if for no other reason,
to get her pen moving.

TEN CHAIRS

For Jason Ryberg

Write ten poems about a chair,
ten different chairs, or one chair
in ten different rooms, ten different people,
ten chairs abandoned.

Ten chairs broken, like the time
you plopped down on an heirloom
in Tyler's apartment, ten useless chairs,
ten-used-to-be chairs.

Ten executions in an electric chair,
ten bodies burned, wasted,
hung up on revenge.
Ten stories of broken systems,
ten chairs holding nine justices
and one chairman, the committee
for briefcases full of hundred dollar bills
and ivory towers topped with little chairs.

Ten monologues to a vacant chair,
the dark stuff, tickled throats
and a transatlantic accent
talking beyond the grave
to someone who used to sit in this chair.

The director in a canvass-backed chair,
picturing ten different angles,
ten ways to put light on James Stewart,

bound by his broken leg
and curious lens.
Ten city halls finally installing
handicapped spaces and wheelchair ramps.

Ten torsos bent over chairs,
anonymous sex and Heimlich maneuvers
saving lives wherever people
are willing to put things in their mouths in a hurry.

Ten camping chairs, a bonfire,
ten bottles of happy tidings and
ten more after that, being lifted
to how damp and happy they are,
to how sweet the river tastes,
how good it feels to wash the day away
and relax in a chair.

PORCHING IT UP

for Caleb

It's cold enough to blow smoke rings without the cigars,
but I'm not above suffering a little.
Remember the time we invented wisdom,
cracked our heads open and looked up,
gathered all the problems of the world
into one utterable sum? I don't, either,
but I feel like we can try.
A freezing gust of epiphany,
sage directions for the hunt,
the golden words of impossibly old men
hovering in our vaulted skulls
like steam, escaping however it can.

IN WHICH JERA IS PRACTICALLY IMPOSSIBLE TO DESCRIBE

Precocious isn't the right word, as it assumes there's anything left for you to know, a time you're not already ahead of. Stable implies there was once a plane you couldn't stand on, that any grid, no matter the dimensions, could ever expect to hold you. Some words would work, because you are smart, you are funny, but what is being gained in describing something by its own standard. It's like saying, "Look, a waterfall, you can tell by its waterfall-ness" but you know me, every sentence becomes a contest and no one ever won the room by being repetitive. I am NOT going to start using the same word twice in the same sentence.

LEGAL SUNRISE

Rising early.
Weary-eyed moments
of thanksgiving.

Flick on the switch,
defer to the list,
things I couldn't do before I got sober:

greet the morning with obedience,
glance into the gun cabinet
without dreaming of sulfur and soiled curtains.

Preparation lights up the senses.
Blaze orange, hazelnut coffee,
a sunrise that creeps alongside the highway,
a chill that calls you, keeps you mobile.

These are the wonders of God, small joys.
marvelous things worth waking up for.

MY DEAD BROTHER TAKES ME FISHING

Chicken livers and a soft breeze.
He baits his hook with his smoking hand,
draws deep. Two lungs able
to swallow death and sing praise
in one cool breath.

Heaven's treasury repleted,
he comes armed with crankbait
coated in platinum, encrusted with rubies,
but they still aren't biting.

At least now, he waits through the doldrum.
He is able to hold onto a little silence.
No mysterious bulges in his pocket,
not a single excuse to cut out early, go home
and further pollute his arterial streams.

We've got an eternity's worth of time,
decent company, and the wind.
A big brown bag stuffed full of turkey sandwiches.

UNTITLED

I cry Amersterdam, heaving
great green aventurine sobs.
I look for rivers and immediately
judge their mudden mouths to be
too bloated with poor brown salt,
too here. I consider improvement,
tying sickles to my wrists
then bolting through cornfields, making room
for tulips, bridges
that carry and suspend us where breath
ceases to need a lung's resistance,
where we appreciate the city's smells
on their last reach upward.
Just a high, cold place to die, to lie down,
dream of curved brick forever.

IN CHICAGO, TOO

In neon dives
   of carpet, movies,
   and strung out singers...
In blue-lit couches
   and snack cake comas...
In concrete stretches of America
   outlined with grease and styrofoam.
   Yellow lense of 5 pm:
   whistle teeth smokes,
   dinner breath,
   the forced posture of awake.
   All night, dog.
   Navy lens of 5 am:
   sore neck
   and the kind of conversation that floors before it kills.
In blonde-covered books
   and black and white screens...
In slick pages full of drawings:
   energy, explosions, and death...
In Italian, Japanese, and English tales
   of country and crime...
In vinyl...
In tape...
In plastic wrapped diamond...
In voyage-long depths of helvetica
   with the sad-eyed heroines of all fiction
   and their glossy counterparts.
In the bumbling hands of has-been professors and their
   prodigies...

In the one and only survivors of a gender gone wrong,
  or so I like to think.
  Congratulations comes so easy.
In the white and gray wash beneath a chat room...
In the shelves of industry...
In the good intentions of artist types: ink and power and
money and filth...
In the dank stems of city growth...
In basements...
In slick cushioned avenue lounges...
In the pigeon worn houses of loft, lull, and future...
In cotton and silk...
In the incline rest of quick and secret love...
In bed...
In the crumbling churches of Indiana and Kansas
  rosaries hanging unblessed and crosses,
  wooden, homemade crosses,
  mark a birth, death, baptism, or marriage.
In the power suits of Washington
  and her marble steps...
In glass cases...
In hipster propaganda and true classics...
In the 90s...
In the rasp of a deservedly wounded girl and her best
  friend's keyboard:
  bright and foamy voices
  singing sarcastic ballads, chronicling all the shit I've
  done before.
In hurt, in print
  the philosophy thereof.
In Rousseau and Bastiat...
In French reminders...

In femininity out of reach...
In red and yellow posters
    (I swear I threw them away).
In the hot stone press of creation...
In denim, that working class chic...
In shark hunter ships and row boats...
In rivers...
In sand...
In grass...
In grain...
In out-of-town-houses and social adventure
    where you win the title-bearing drop
    of a girl's eyes, I am cool, now.
In the books I didn't read...
In the temples I didn't have the courage to pray in...
In distant hearts and missed opportunities...
I saw where and where I wished I came from
and somehow became a person.

IN WHICH JERA IS MY ONLY FRIEND WHO
BUYS MY BOOK

It's best, I suppose.
The way most people shake their heads,
blanch at the sight of feelings as ink on paper.

I remember that poem Brent wrote,
the one about his pen and its propensity for romance,
for the color red as it takes every form imaginable,
every possible red reference in the poetic lexicon.

It's a strange thing, our ability to judge,
to look at the world and feel as if my perspective
is worth the life of a tree, the gears in a printer,
and some poor artist, to snap a picture
and tack my name to it. To feel as if I have the authority
to hold someone else's work up to the light
and dismiss its derivative use of shade.
Poets spend too much time guessing, wondering
who their readers might be, what makes them
pull out their wallets and take a gamble,
that what I spend my whole life crying about
is worth an hour or two of their day.
Me? I know exactly who my reader is,
and I know exactly what I'll say next.

Timothy Tarkelly is a poet and educator from Southeast Kansas. His work has appeared in *Words and Whispers, The Red Lemon Review,* and *As It Ought To Be Magazine.* He's published several books of poetry including *A Horse Called Victory* (Kelsay Books), *Objects We Know We Don't Deserve: Poems on Dutch Art* (Alien Buddha Press), *On Slip Rigs and Spiritual Growth* (OAC Books), *Luckhound* (Spartan Press), and others. He recently collaborated with Elena Samarsky, a Ukrainian visual artist, on a work of paintings and poems entitled *All Other Forms of Expression* (OAC Books). When he's not writing, he teaches English and Speech to students who are much more talented than he is.

This project was made possible, in part, by generous support from the Osage Arts Community.

Osage Arts Community provides temporary time, space and support for the creation of new artistic works in a retreat format, serving creative people of all kinds — visual artists, composers, poets, fiction and nonfiction writers. Located on a 152-acre farm in an isolated rural mountainside setting in Central Missouri and bordered by ¾ of a mile of the Gasconade River, OAC provides residencies to those working alone, as well as welcoming collaborative teams, offering living space and workspace in a country environment to emerging and mid-career artists. For more information, visit us at www.osageac.org

Osage Arts Community